THE BURIED CITIES OF CEYLON
A Guide Book to Anuradhapura and Polonaruwa

MAVEN BOOKS

THE BURIED CITIES OF CEYLON
A Guide Book to Anuradhapura and Polonaruwa

S.M. Burrows

&

M.A. Oxon

Ceylon Civil Service

MAVEN BOOKS

Chennai   **Trichy**   **Tirunelveli**   **New Delhi**

MAVEN BOOKS

An Imprint of **MJP Publishers**

ISBN 978-93-87867-07-9   **MAVEN BOOKS**

All rights reserved   No. 44, Nallathambi Street, Triplicane, Chennai 600 005

MJP 573   © Publishers, 2020

Publisher: **C. Janarthanan**

This book has been published in good faith that the work of the author is original. All efforts have been taken to make the material error-free. However, the author and publisher disclaim responsibility for any inadvertent errors.

PUBLISHER'S NOTE

The legacy of a country is in its varied cultural heritage, historical literature, developments in the field of economy and science. The top nations in the world are competing in the field of science, economy and literature. This vast legacy has to be conserved and documented so that it can be bestowed to the future generation. The knowledge of this legacy is slowly getting perished in the present generation due to lack of documentation.

Keeping this in mind, the concern with retrospective acquiring of rare books has been accented recently by the burgeoning reprint industry. Maven Books is gratified to retrieve the rare collections with a view to bring back those books that were landmarks in their time.

In this effort, a series of rare books would be republished under the banner, "Maven Books". The books in the reprint series have been carefully selected for their contemporary usefulness as well as their historical importance within the intellectual. We reconstruct the book with slight enhancements made for better presentation, without affecting the contents of the original edition.

Most of the works selected for republishing covers a huge range of subjects, from history to anthropology. We believe this reprint edition will be a service to the numerous researchers and practitioners active in this fascinating field. We allow readers to experience the wonder of peering into a scholarly work of the highest order and seminal significance.

MAVEN BOOKS

PREFACE.

THIS little book does not profess to contain anything strikingly original: its aim is to introduce the traveller and the antiquarian (and the two are frequently synonymous), to rarely trodden and most fascinating ground ; to the beautiful remains of an architecture and a civilization of 2,000 years ago, the greater part of which are easily accessible: and to make a humble attempt at awakening, if possible, a greater interest in a part of Ceylon which is only just arising from the slumber and neglect of many centuries. There is an abundance of able works on Ceylon, some of which deal more or less completely with the "buried cities;" but none of them are of very recent date, nor do they contain such practical information as will help the traveller to form an idea of the task that lies before him. That task has been rendered comparatively easy by the improvements of advancing civilization. The best months for seeing the "buried cities" (January and February) correspond exactly with

the time when the stream of visitors through Ceylon is
naturally the largest ; and a week of ordinary travel will
introduce the visitor to an artistic and archæological treat
which is perhaps unique in the East, and will enable him
to arrive at a very different estimate of the past history of
the Sinhalese race from that which he would form, were
he to confine himself to the beaten tracks of Kandy and
Colombo.   The voluble vendors of expensive tortoiseshell
and fallacious gems are not fair representatives of a
nation which could build a city of gigantic monoliths,
carve a mountain into a graceful shrine, and decorate its
pious monuments with delicate pillars that would have
done credit to a Grecian artist.

My warmest thanks are due to Mr. H. C. P. Bell, c.c.s.,
Archæological Commissioner ; but for whose generous
permission to make free use of his valuable Reports and
papers, the present edition of this work would be of little
value.

S. M. B.

May, 1899.

ILLUSTRATIONS.

CONTENTS.

INDEX.

ERRATA :—On page 4, line 8 from bottom, "dentical" should be "*identical*." Page 8, line 2, *delete* "t" after "Dambulia." Page 18, line 11, "Hahindu" should be "*Mahindu*."

PART I.
HISTORICAL.

PART I.

HISTORICAL.

IT is a remarkable fact that although the Sinhalese do not rank as a literary nation, and have not produced a single author with any claim to world-wide eminence, they have the peculiar distinction of possessing a series of chronicles, of unimpeached authenticity, which narrate their history from their earliest landing in the island down to the last century. A full account of these chronicles (which are collectively known as the " Mahawanso," or " Genealogy of the Great ") will be found in the well-known work of Sir Emerson Tennent on Ceylon.* It is sufficient to say here that they were begun in A.D. 460, by a Buddhist priest named Mahanamo, uncle of the reigning monarch, Dhátu Séna ; and his work, which comprised the period between B.C. 543, when the Sinhalese, led by Wijeyo, first reached Ceylon, and A.D. 301, was carried down by various monastic successors to the commencement of the British rule.

* 4th Ed., Vol. I., Pt. iii., ch. 1.

Being written in Pali verse, these chronicles were a sealed book, until, in 1826, Mr. George Turnour, a Ceylon Civil Servant, was fortunate enough to obtain possession of the running commentary usually written by the Pali authors to explain the obscurities of their poetry ; and with the help of this he was able to publish a translation of the most important portion of these unique annals. Such knowledge as we have, therefore, of the history of the buried cities of Ceylon, is entirely due to his admirable perseverance and erudition.   An English translation of these remarkable chronicles was made by L. C. Wijesinghe Mudaliyar under instructions from the late Governor of Ceylon, the Hon. Sir Arthur Gordon (Lord Stanmore) and forms not the least worthy monument of a memorable rule.

It is a moot point how much confidence is to be placed in the early chronology of the island, as detailed in these annals. The landing of Wijeyo and his Sinhalese followers is placed suspiciously near to the date of the Nirvána of Gautama Buddha as reckoned in Ceylon; and it is remarkable that the original invaders were able to erect so perfect an architectural monument as the Thûpârâma within 150 years from their first invasion. Still greater obscurity surrounds the question as to the origin of the Sinhalese, and of the aborigines whom they ousted and superseded. A dim tradition (supported by the early Portuguese historians and by Pridham*), points to a Siamese or Malay origin for one or both races ; but as proof is entirely wanting to support it, it is safer to suppose that both races found their way to the island from the neighbouring continent. All we can confidently

---

* Vol. I., ch. iii., p. 24.

say of the aborigines is, that they were a rude race, who left no monuments or records behind them ; that they were probably forced to do serf-labour for their Sinhalese conquerors ; that most of them became gradually absorbed into the dominant race ; but that a remnant of them carried on the struggle for a considerable time ; and, preferring a wild forest life to qualified slavery, are still to be traced in the almost extinct Veddâs.*

In B.C. 543, Wijeyo and his Sinhalese followers landed in Ceylon, possibly near the modern Puttalam on the west coast.† He is said to have been the discarded son of one of the petty princes in the valley of the Ganges, while the native chronicles explain the name of his race by tracing his paternity to a lion (Sinha). He conquered the aborigines (" demons," as they are called in the chronicle), chiefly by the help of one of their princesses, Kuweni, whom he married and afterwards repudiated in order to ally himself with the daughter of an Indian Râjah,‡ and settled his followers in various parts of the island. After a reign of 39 years, he was succeeded by his nephew Panduwasa, who also sought a wife from the Indian continent. This princess brought her six brothers with her, who soon formed settlements for themselves ; one of them, Wijita, building Wijitapura or Vigitapura,§ and another, Anuradha, the city which still bears his name. This city was eventually chosen as

* For an account of the Veddâs, see Tennent's Ceylon, Vol. II., Pt. ix., ch. 3.

† Mr. H. Parker plausibly argues for a landing on the S.-E. coast, near Tisamaharâma. See Royal Asiatic Society's Journal for 1884.

‡ An interesting note to ch. 2, part iii. of Tennent's Ceylon traces the analogy between this and that of Ulysses and Circe.

§ See Part ii., ch. 4.

his capital by the reigning monarch, and was greatly enlarged and beautified by his successor, Pandukhabayo, who ascended the throne about B.C. 437. The native chronicles give an interesting account of this monarch's administrative efforts, which should gain him the respect of modern apostles of sanitation. He appointed 150 men to carry dead bodies to the cemetery, and 150 men as cemetery-keepers and sextons. There were 200 night-soil men, a large number of night and day guards, and a small army of sweepers. The Vẹddâs were placed in a separate settlement near the town, and in the same neighbourhood settlements were made for naked mendicants and fakirs, and for the " castes of the heathen."

But the more practical achievements of Pandukhabayo pale before the pious renown of his successor, King Tisa (or Dewenipiatisa), the Henry VI. of Sinhalese annals, who came to the throne about B.C. 306. It was in his reign that the royal missionary Mahindo, son of the Indian King Dharmasoka, landed in Ceylon, and either introduced or regenerated Buddhism.* The monarch and all his court, his consort and all her women, became ready converts to the new tenets; the arrival of Mahindo's sister, Sanghamittâ with a branch of the dentical tree under which Gautama obtained Buddhahood, consummated the conversion of the island; and the King devoted the rest of his reign to the erection of enormous monuments, rock temples, and monasteries to mark his zeal for the new faith. Of these, the Thûpârâma, the Isurumuniya, and some of the buildings at Mihintale still attest his piety, his munificence, and his command of labour. He died in the odour of sanctity

---

* See Part ii., ch. 3.

after a reign of 40 years. Four princes succeeded him, whose reigns were unimportant, save for the fact that one of them, Suratisa, took into his pay a mercenary force of Malabars, who were the forerunners of those frequent invaders who gradually expelled the Sinhalese from the whole of the Northern section of the island.

It would be a mistake to suppose that these Malabars (or 'Damilos,' as they are called in the chronicle) were precisely the people now known by that name. They were chiefly the inhabitants of the great South Indian Kingdom of Pâṇḍya, and some of them came from places as far north as Orissa and Cuttack. The two leaders of the mercenaries employed by Suratisa succeeded in murdering that monarch, and seizing, for a time, the supreme power ; and it was their success that brought on the first great invasion of Ceylon in B.C. 204, under the illustrious Eláḷa, a prince of Mysore. Landing in the country when the sceptre was in the weak grasp of an irresolute king, Eláḷa met with such success, that he was able, not only to seize the throne, but to maintain himself there for a space of 30 years. Whether this long reign was the reward of a just and wise rule, or the result of a tacit acquiescence on the part of an unwarlike people in his claims to the sovereignty, it is hard to say ; but even the bigoted chronicler admits that he " administered justice impartially to friend and foe."

It is at least not difficult to see that seldom can an easier prey than Anuradhapura have fallen to a conqueror's hand. Situated on a level plain, without one single natural advantage of mountain, river or forest, the position was strategically indefensible unless by a warlike and determined people. This, however, was precisely

what the Sinhalese were not : they were agricultural
rather than bellicose, better at building bunds than at
raising redoubts ; while the available force of the kingdom,
instead of being trained in the arts of war, was directed
by their monarchs towards the construction of those
gigantic dágobas, which were thus at once the glory and
the ruin of the realm.

But the legitimate royal family had still a worthy
representative left in Prince Dutugẹmunu, and the contest
for the sovereignty between him and Eláḷa, which was
fought about B.C. 164, forms the most striking tale of
chivalry in Sinhalese history. The final battle, which
took place outside the walls of Anuradhapura, was for a
long time doubtful, until it was decided by a single contest between the two leaders, each mounted on a huge
elephant ; the usurper was defeated and slain, and the
rightful heir was hailed king on the field of battle.
Satiated with military success, and penitent for the
bloodshed he had caused, he determined to devote the
rest of his life to expiatory acts of religion. But his first
care was to erect a generous and fitting monument to his
rival Eláḷa, and to enact that the music of processions
should cease, and kings alight from their palanquins, as
they passed the tomb. The site of this is supposed to be
marked at the present day by a conical mound of earth ;
nor was the generous enactment less lasting ; for in 1816,
as Pilamé Taláwé, the head of the leading Kandyan clan
was escaping through Anuradhapura after an unsuccessful
attempt at insurrection, he is said to have alighted from
his litter, weary as he was, and walked on until he was
well past the venerable memorial.

The pious king next set about the erection of the Ruwanvęlisęya, the proudest work of his reign, which is said to have been originally 270 feet high, and to contain (or to have contained) innumerable costly offerings and relics of Buddha ; of the Lowa Mahâ Pâya, or Brazen Palace, with its foundation of 1,600 granite pillars, its nine stories, and 900 chambers for priests ; of the Mirisvętiya dágoba ; the " stone canoe " and other stupendous works. His end is touchingly described by the priestly chronicler. During his last illness he caused himself to be carried to a couch placed opposite to the Ruwanvęlisęya (the site is supposed to be marked by a granite slab to the present day), that he might fix his expiring gaze on his grandest achievement. An attendant priest recited his many deeds of piety and munificence. " All these acts," replied the monarch, " done in my days of prosperity, afford no comfort to my mind : but two offerings which I made when in affliction and adversity regardless of my own fate, are those which alone solace me now." His eyes are closed with a benediction from the priest. " Thus," moralizes the partial chronicler, " do the truly wise obtain for themselves imperishable and most profitable rewards from their otherwise perishable and useless wealth."

The reigns of the four Râjas who followed are unimportant ; but King Walagam Báhu, who came to the throne in B.C. 104, poses as a champion of the faith only inferior to Tissa and Dutugemunu. Barely a year after his accession, the second great invasion of the Malabars took place, forcing the King to seek safety in flight, and to hide in dens and caves of the rocks. When he regained his throne, after a long exile of 15 years, he transformed many of these rocky asylums into elaborate temples,

the most notable among them being the rock temples of
Dambullat.* Another of his asylums, the Aḷuvihára caves
near Mátale, was rendered still more illustrious in a
different way. About B.C. 90, the King assembled there
a company of monks, and caused the Buddhist scriptures,
which had been orally delivered by Mahindo, and afterwards preserved by tradition, to be transcribed into Pali,
and thus fixed for ever. The third great act of his reign
was the erection of the Abhayagiriya ("mountain of
safety") dágoba, the most stupendous work in Ceylon,
as it originally stood 405 feet from the ground. It appears
to have had a larger body of priests attached to it than any
of the other shrines, and, later on, was a notable strong-
hold of the Wytulian heresy. The King died in B.C. 77.

It would be unprofitable to weary the reader with
even an epitome of the reigns of the uninteresting Rájas
who successively "raised the canopy of dominion" at
Anuradhapura. They most of them built tanks, suffered
more or less from the constant invasions of the Malabars,
and ended an inglorious life with a violent death. Irrigation, subjugation, assassination, may be said to form a
trilogy of incidents monotonously frequent. The monotony is broken by the misdeeds of a wicked queen, the
" infamous Anula "—the Messalina of Sinhalese annals—
whose taste for paramours was as varied as her operations
with poison were successful ; and by a monarch, Bhâtiya
Tisa, whose piety was so exemplary, that he, alone of
laymen, was allowed to pass through the secret passage of
Ruwanvęli dágoba and gaze on the wondrous relics and
offerings that filled the inmost chamber. Of the rest,
twenty-two were killed by their successors, six by others,

* See Part ii., ch. 1.

thirteen fell in war, four committed suicide, eleven were dethroned and disappeared. Meanwhile Buddhism flourished amazingly, and largely increased its influence and possessions. Wide districts, fertilized perhaps by the interception of a river and the formation of suitable canals, were appropriated to the use of the local priesthood ; a tank, with the thousands of acres it watered, was sometimes assigned for the perpetual repair of a dágoba.

The third great invasion of the Malabars took place about A.D. 106, and the invaders succeeded in carrying back with them, not only vast quantities of plunder, but also 12,000 Sinhalese captives. King Gaja Báhu, however, in A.D. 112, conducted an expedition to the continent, released the captives, and carried back an equal number of prisoners to Ceylon.

But other than mere carnal foes were shortly to gain a foothold in the island. From the very beginning of the third century A.D., a schismatic sect had begun to put forward the doctrines known as the Wytulian heresy ; but their attempts had twice been frustrated, and the heretics ignominiously punished. What the exact tenets of this heresy were, the chronicles do not enlighten us ; but it was possibly an attempt of the Brahmins of India to oust Buddhism from Ceylon by the same tactics which they had so successfully used on the continent. In the reign of Gothábaya (A.D. 248) it again made a bid for dominion, and one of its most eminent, though secret, adherents got himself appointed tutor to the king's two sons. The younger of these, Mahá Séna, fully profited by the lessons he received, and when he came to the throne, in A.D. 275, set to work at once to supplant the old creed by the new. He forbade the bestowal of offerings on the adherents of the old religion, who were thus forced by hunger and want to fly to the south of the island ; he razed to the ground the Brazen Palace and over 300 other buildings, and devoted their materials to the erection of shrines for the new cult. But the *vox populi* was strongly opposed to these innovations ; the King was not so well supported as was Henry VIII. under somewhat similar circumstances, and was forced to avoid, by a timely and complete recantation, the threatened dangers of general insurrection. He sacrificed his tutor, Sangha-mitra, and his chief supporter among the nobles, to the popular frenzy, rebuilt the edifices he had destroyed, recalled the priests, and devoted the rest of his reign to the erection of gigantic monuments of his new-born orthodoxy. Of these the most conspicuous was the Jetawanáráma dágoba—still the most picturesque and massive ruin in Anuradhapura—which originally was 316, and is still 269, feet high ; while the most useful was the great tank at Minnéri,* twenty miles in circumference, which was connected by a canal with the large tanks of Kanthalai or Gantalawa, and Kowdelly. He also formed sixteen other tanks, and repaired numerous temples : " and," says the writer of the Maháwanso, " his destiny after death was according to his merits." A vast amount of fable and superstition clustered around the name of the deceased monarch, who is called in the chronicles " the last of the Maháwanso,"—the great solar dynasty. The country was visited after his death by a series of bad seasons and disastrous epidemics : the people turned to the memory of the mighty Rája, and implored his pro-tection or deprecated his wrath with prayers and offer-

* See Part ii., ch. 5.

ings; sickness and famine gradually abated; and his grateful worshippers hailed him as " Minnéri Deviyó " or " Hat Rajjuruvó," while his shrine at Minnéri came to be regarded with peculiar awe and veneration.

The reign of his son, Kirrti Ṣri Megahawarna, (A.D. 202) was made illustrious by the arrival from Dantapura, in India (probably the modern Juggernath), of the celebrated Daḷadá relic, the sacred tooth of Buddha.* The King of Kálinga (the modern Orissa), being unable to defend it from the fanatical attacks of the Brahmins, sent it for safekeeping to Ceylon in the charge of his son and daughter, concealed in the folds of his daughter's hair. A shrine, known as the Daḷadá Máligawa, was built for it near the Thúpáráma dágoba, and a similar shrine of exquisite workmanship received it at Polonnaruwa when the older city was finally vacated.

It was during the reign of his fourth successor, Mahá-náma, who ascended the throne A.D. 410, that Anuradhapura was visited by the celebrated Chinese traveller, Fa Hian, whose writings are independent evidence of, and strongly corroborate, the truth of the Sinhalese chronicles. He describes the broad, straight streets, the beautiful public buildings, the mountain-like monuments of Buddha, the aspect of the Bo-tree (which is almost literally applicable to its present condition) ; and the ceremonies which attended the exhibition of the sacred tooth. It was about this time, too, that Ceylon first entered into political relations with China, and paid tribute to that country for over 100 years. Nor was intercourse with the West entirely unknown at this epoch. Ammianus Marcellinus

---

* For an account of the tooth relic, see " The Visitor's Guide to Kandy," by the same author.

asserts that an embassy was sent from Ceylon to the court of the Emperor Julian in the reign of Mahánáma's predecessor, King Upatissa II; while Pliny makes mention of a still earlier embassy to Italy, which was dispatched in the reign of King Chanda-Mukha-Siwa, A.D. 44-52.

A long period of Malabar oppression followed the demise of King Mahánáma, the invaders being finally ejected, after a prolonged struggle, by King Dhátu Séna, who mounted the throne A.D. 459. It was at his instance that the Maháwaṇso was compiled by his uncle and tutor, Mahánámo Terunnánse, and carried down to the death of Mahasen; and it was this monarch who constructed the enormous tank of Kalávewa.* But his end was a tragic one. He had married his daughter to his nephew, who grossly insulted her; and in revenge the King caused his nephew's mother to be burned. Incensed by this, his nephew and his eldest son raised the standard of rebellion, seized the King's person, and pressed him to reveal his hidden treasures. The King undertook to do so, if he were allowed to visit once more his great tank of Kalávewa, and speak with his early friend, the priest Mahánámo. He was accordingly sent thither, in a mean cart with broken wheels, and under a strong guard. Arrived there, he received much spiritual consolation from the priest, and much bodily consolation from bathing in and drinking the waters; and pointing to his friend and to the tank, exclaimed that these were the only treasures he possessed. Carried back to the capital, he was stripped naked, cast into chains, and built up and embedded in a wall, and Kásyapa, his son, reigned in his stead. "What

* See Part ii., ch. 4.

wise man," (comments the chronicler) "would covet riches, life or prosperity after this?" But parricide proved an insecure foundation for dominion. After an unsuccessful attempt to murder his younger brother, Mogallána, who fled to India, Kásyapa feared to live in his open capital, and having strongly fortified the already inaccessible rock of Sígiri,* repaired thither, deposited his treasures, and built a palace. In vain he tried to expiate his crime by enriching temples, by forming public gardens, by taking the strictest vows of self-mortification. His avenging brother, returning from India with an army, enticed the parricide to leave his fortress and risk an engagement near Ambatthalo in the Seven Korales. In the middle of the battle, the King turned aside his elephant to avoid a swamp : thinking he was flying, his followers threw down their arms in despair; and the avenger with his own hand struck off the head of his impious brother.

The tragic end of Mogallána's successor, Kumára Dás (A.D. 515), is worthy of record. One night, when in the house of a courtesan, the King wrote a riddle on the wall, promising to him who could interpret it the fulfilment of any request he might proffer. The celebrated Indian poet, Pandita Kálidás, visited the courtesan's house soon afterwards, and answered the riddle ; but the courtesan, wishing to keep for herself the renown and the reward, murdered the poet, buried him under her house, and claimed the authorship of the answer. The King, incredulous and suspicious, caused search to be made ; the body of Kálidás was discovered, the murderess put to death, and a huge funeral pile was raised to cremate the poet's remains.

* See Part ii., ch. 6.

When the flames were at their height, the King, struck with remorse at the irreparable loss, rushed into the fire and was burned; and his five queens immediately followed his example and were consumed with him.

The reigns of the succeeding monarchs were marked by continual civil discord and Malabar encroachments: until in A.D. 769, King Aggrabódhi IV. found it necessary to fly from the obnoxious invaders, evacuate Anuradhapura, and establish a new capital at Polonnaruwa. Previous kings had selected this spot as an occasional residence: in A.D. 368 King Upatisa II. had formed the tank of Topávewa in its immediate vicinity; and in A.D. 650 King Siri Sangabo II. built a palace there. The new city was soon furnished with the necessary means of irrigation, and ornamented with vast religious structures; but the change of capital only served to increase the strength and influence of the Malabars. Each successive monarch held the reins of power with a feebler grasp; famine and disease decimated the country, and Buddhism declined; until in A.D. 1023, the Malabars seized the person of the reigning monarch, carried him, his queen, and his treasures, to India, and established a Malabar Viceroy at Polonnaruwa. The fortunes of the Sinhalese monarchy were at their lowest ebb, but were destined to revive once more, and for the last time. The royal family had taken refuge in Ruhuna, in the south of the island, and a prince of the name of Wijeya Báhu was there crowned King of Ceylon in A.D. 1071. He soon showed signs of warlike energy, collected a force, marched against Polonnaruwa, and defeating the Malabars outside its walls, took the city by storm. His efforts to raise the magnificence of the city, reform the priesthood, and re-establish justice and

order were interrupted by a second contest with the
Malabars, who, victorious this time, again seized the city,
and razed the palace to the ground. The undaunted
king, however, once more besieged the invaders, drove
them to the coast, and even perpetrated a short invasion
of the country of his hereditary foes. He died in A.D.
1126, and was eventually succeeded in A.D. 1153, by his
grandson, Parákrama Báhu, who is almost the only notable character of the Polonnaruwan epoch. The early
part of his reign was marked by a series of struggles with
foes of his own household, from which he emerged
triumphant into undisputed sovereignty. Returning to
his capital, he devoted himself to the arts of peace, the
restoration of religion, and the expansion of architecture.
He sent to Siam for priests of the superior rank, which
was nearly extinct in the island; and he summoned a
Church Council to settle debatable questions of religion ;
he restored the sacred edifices of Anuradhapura, he
built innumerable "Wiharas," preaching-halls, and rock
temples ; the most remarkable of these rock shrines, the
Galwihara at Polonnaruwa, being at the present day in
very much the same state as it is described in the Maháwanso. He also placed guards round the coast and
erected fortresses of refuge, raised a wall round the
capital which is said to have enclosed an area twelve
miles broad by nearly thirty long, built almonries for the
poor at the four gates, and a palace for himself with
4,000 apartments, constructed 1,470 new tanks, and
repaired as many old ones. A fresh revolt of his domestic
foes again summoned him to the battle-field, and he
celebrated his final victory by a magnificent procession
which reads like a Roman triumph. The heavenly
powers smiled upon his success ; for a heavy storm broke

while the triumph was in progress, and furious rain flooded all the ground but that occupied by the procession, which remained miraculously dry. He next turned his arms against the Kings of Cambodia and Arramana (a region lying between Siam and Arracan), who had plundered his merchants and insulted his ambassador. In a pitched battle, his general defeated and slew the Cambodian King, seized his capital, and made the country tributary to his royal master. A second expedition was shortly afterwards dispatched against the allied monarchs of Soli and Páṇḍi, whose headquarters were at Madura in South India. Success again attended the Sinhalese arms ; the enemy, in spite of their overwhelming numbers, were repulsed and broken in seven great battles ; Rameswaram and the six neighouring districts fell into the victor's hands, and Páṇḍi paid tribute to Polonnaruwa. The mere recital of these exploits of war and peace, while it fills us with admiration for the last great prince of a fading race, gives us some idea of the command of labour, the density of population, the activity of agriculture in a land which is now a wilderness of barren jungle inhabited by a few fever-stricken villagers. Parákrama Báhu died in A.D. 1186, in the thirty-third year of his reign. A characteristic statue, commonly assigned to this king, still stands, cut from a solitary rock, about a mile and a half to the south of the city which owed to him all its glory. The King has his back turned to the city, and holds in his hand the open "book of the law," as if to imply that more consolation is to be found in religious meditation than in the construction of many monuments.

With this great monarch's reign the power and prestige of the Sinhalese monarchy virtually terminates.

King Kirti Nissanga, who came to the throne in A.D. 1192, gained high renown by the attention he devoted to religious edifices. He repaired and enlarged the rock temples of Dambulla, and caused the huge Galpota, or inscribed stone, twenty-five feet long by four broad and two thick, to be carried by his "strong men" from Mihintale to Polonnaruwa, a distance of over 80 miles. After his death, the clouds of invasion closed in thick and fast over the ill-fated realm. In A.D. 1219 a huge expedition of 24,000 men from the Northern Circars overran the land, placed their leader on the throne, tortured and mutilated the inhabitants, and destroyed a large number of Buddhist monuments, making the island, says the chronicle, "like a house filled with fire or thieves." They were destined never to be again ejected. In A.D. 1240 the seat of Government had to be transferred to Dambadeniya, and thence to Yápahu, to Kurunégala, to Gampola, to Kandy, and finally to Cotta, near Colombo ; and it was at this latter place that news was brought to the King, (A.D. 1552) that a ship had anchored near Colombo containing "a race of men surpassingly white and beautiful, wearing boots and hats of iron, eating a white stone and drinking blood, and having guns which could break a castle of marble." But with the landing of the Portuguese, and the vast importance of its results, we have nothing to do ; the "great cities" of the Empire were deserted or in the hands of foreigners, the great tanks were broken and their fields lay barren, the Sinhalese monarchy existed but in name, when the white man landed on the coast, destined ultimately to restore fresh energies to the dwindling race, and create for it a new and nobler history of progress and civilization.

D

Two or three general questions will naturally occur to the traveller who explores these magnificent ruins :—

I. Who were the artists whose skill and taste in sculpture are to be found over such an extensive area ? It must be remembered that though the Sinhalese and Tamils are ethnologically distinct races, the connexion between them was, from the earliest ages, very close. The two first rájas sought wives from the Indian continent ; their new acquisitions were colonized by Indian adventurers ; and the religion of the island was, until the arrival of the Buddhist missionary Hahindu, probably Hinduistic to a very large degree.   The traveller who has visited the great shrines and ruins of Southern India, more especially the Seven Pagodas, south of Madras, cannot fail to be struck by the similarity of many cf the characteristics of Anuradhapuran (and, still more clearly Polonnaruwan) architecture with the carvings to be found on the continent.   Whatever the date of these latter may be, it seems more rational to suppose that both the designs and the artists came from the continent to Ceylon than *vice versa*.   Moreover, the Sinhalese, both educated and uneducated, are ready to allow that the sculptors were imported Tamils ; and the existence of several villages of Tamil " gaJ-waduwas " (stone-carvers) seems to confirm this admission. Further, if the Sinhalese were the artists, it is curious that all traces of the art should have utterly died out among them ; while that the Tamils are most cunning sculptors to the present day, is amply proved by many parts of the great Madura temple, which were executed almost within the memory of living man.   The only difficulty is that the design of the pillars, which play so important a part in the Sinhalese ruins, appears to be confined to the island, but the ornaments on their capitals are obviously Hindu. Even the sacred goose is to be found in a precisely similar form among the animals represented on the celebrated carving at the Seven Pagodas known as the Penance of Arjuna. It is just possible that the absence of all remains of carving-tools, chisels, &c., is to be accounted for by the fact that as most of the skilled workmen were imported from the continent, they carried their tools away with them when they returned to their own land. Lastly, it is distinctly stated in the Mahá-waṇso that King Prákrama Báhu (A.D. 1115) " brought Damilo artificers " from the opposite coast of India to decorate Polonnaruwa, and no comment is made on this as an unusual proceeding.

II. Where did the stone come from, and how was it transported ? The stone used in the ruins is nearly all granite and syenite, with a small proportion of limestone. Most of this was found in the immediate neighbourhood of the town ; nearly all the layers of rock which crop up in several places in the surrounding jungles bearing marks of the wedges by means of which the pillars and large blocks were detached. Elephants were probably employed to transport these heavy weights ; though, as we know from the chronicles that wheeled vehicles were in use, they may also have been carried on trucks dragged by large bodies of men, after the manner of the Ninevite paintings. How such a weighty mass as the stone canopy* was raised into position without (so far as we know) the aid of cranes and pulleys, it is hard to say.

* See Part ii., ch. I.

It is possible that the sustaining pillars were first placed in position, the space between them filled with earth, an inclined plane (of earth) made from the ground to the top of this mound, the canopy prized up it and placed in position, and the earth dug away from underneath.

III. The state of ruin to which all the buildings are reduced is generally ascribed entirely to the malignity of the Tamils. No doubt a great deal of it is due to their iconoclastic zeal ; but in justice to them it must be remembered that there were two other agents of destruction, less violently aggressive, but more persistent. (1.) Polonnaruwa is a striking instance of the harm that can be done by roots of trees, especially by members of the fig family. A seed finds its way to some crevice or niche, and in a few years the tree which springs from it throws upwards a heavy trunk and branches, and downwards a perfect cataract of snaky roots, which force their way through bricks and between stones, loosen every joint of the building, and eventually bring the whole structure with a crash to the ground. (2.) The Sinhalese, possessed with such weighty notions of a super-structure, had (except in the case of the largest dágobas) the very mildest idea of a foundation. Consequently the great weight above aided and increased the natural subsidence of the earth during many centuries ; and the result is that many of the ruined buildings now look as if they had been displaced by an earthquake.

The exploration of the ruins of the two large cities, so far from being completed, has in reality only just begun. Such as remain of the large and important struc-tures have no doubt been discovered; but equal interest attaches to, and perhaps more information may be gleaned from, the smaller and less obvious fragments and details: every acre that is cleared discloses some of these, and it is not too much to hope that a continued course of intelligent excavation may not only bring to light still more interesting remains, but enable us eventually to form some idea of the shape, dimensions and general appearance of two of the greatest cities of the East.

CHAPTER I.

DAMBULLA.

THE visitor who is wise and enterprising enough to make a pilgrimage to the " buried cities" of Ceylon will leave Kandy for Mátale by train on the first day of his travels. There is a good resthouse here where breakfast or tiffin can be got, if ordered beforehand. Mátale (Post and Telegraph Office) is an exceedingly pretty little town, the capital of the district of Mátale, which is a division of the Central or Kandy Province, and the residence of an Assistant Government Agent and Police Magistrate. The long straggling bazaar, offensive to the nose, is picturesque to the eye, and a large trade is done here both with coolies from the estates around and with the gangs of coolies on the march from South India to find employment in the planting districts.

If he has the afternoon to spare, the visitor, after depositing his baggage at the resthouse, cannot do better than pay a visit to the Aluvihára Temple which is two miles down the main road to the North of Mátale. A guide can be got from the resthouse to show the turn-off. The temple is beautifully situated amid a jungle of gigantic boulders, under the slope of one of which the principal shrine is built. It is remarkable historically as being the place where the sacred words of Buddha were first put into writing. It is worth while going to the very top of the rocks to see the view, which is extensive and characteristic. There are also a carving of Buddha's footprint and a Yantragala or Mystic stone* to be seen there. A horse-coach† leaves Mátale at 5-30 a.m., and, passing through the celebrated coffee and cacao estate of Kawudupelella (6 miles), and the pretty village of Nálande (resthouse, 14 miles) reaches Dambulla (29 miles) about 10 a.m.

As this place contains the largest and most celebrated rock temples in Ceylon, it may be thought worth while to pass the afternoon and night here, and study them. There is a magnificent view to be obtained from the summit of the great rock on which the temples are situated. A guide should be got from the resthouse to point out the little path that leads from the high road to the temple, and notice should be sent to the priest the night before that the keys will be required. Directly after passing a " pansala " or priest's residence, the steep ascent begins, partly up the bare rock and partly up a picturesque stairway. A large brick gateway, called the " Muragé," or guard-house, terminates the ascent, and leads on to the rock-platform in front of the temples. The view to be obtained from this point on a clear morning is hardly equalled in Ceylon. The abrupt peak of Dahiyakande rises up close at hand ; Ratmalegahakande

* See chap. III.

† It is very advisable to write in good time beforehand to the Coach Manager, Mátale, and to all Resthouse-keepers,

forms a conspicuous object to the East ; and range upon range of grey mountains, celebrated in the history of the coffee enterprize, stretch to the horizon in all directions. To the East, the most conspicuous object is the abrupt cylindrical rock of Sígiri,* a most curious example of Sinhalese hill-fortification. Below the rock to the S.-E. lie the rich paddy lands with which a succession of pious rájas endowed the famous shrine.

Probably few temples equal those of Dambulla in meanness of approach : the narrow gallery and coarse modern roofing running under the edge of the overhanging rock form a poor introduction to the impressive interior. Before entering, the visitor should glance upwards at the " Katârê," or ledge formed to keep off the drip of the rain ; on the upper edge of which the remains of an inscription in the oldest form of cave character are still visible. A still more curious and lengthy inscription is to be seen inscribed on the rock to the right, immediately after passing the " Muragé." This describes the reign and the virtues of Rája Kirti Sri Nissanga (A.D. 1192), the most munificent patron of the temples. One passage in it has a familar sound :—" Thrice did he make the circuit of the island, and having visited the villages, the towns and the cities, such was the security he established, as well in the wilderness as in the inhabited places, that even a woman might traverse the country with a precious jewel, and not be asked, what is it ?"

The entrance to the first temple is close to this inscription. The stone doorway is ornamented with a " Makara torana," or ornamental arch. This temple is called the Déwa Rája Vihara (the temple of the great

* See chap. II.

god) ; the title not referring to Buddha but to Vishnu. The interior is very dark, and the eye has to become accustomed to the gloom before it discerns the glory of the shrine—the gigantic recumbent figure of Buddha, which, together with the pillow and couch on which it rests, is cut out of the solid rock, and measures 47 feet in length. The head rests on the right hand, and that again on the pillow, on which is apparent the impression supposed to be made by the head and arm. The soles of the feet are ornamented with lotus-flowers (magul lakunu). Near the head of the statue is a wooden image of Vishnu, and two smaller statues of Buddha made of brick. At the feet is a small Buddha, and a wooden statue of Maha Kâsappa. This shrine is said to have been made by King Walagam Báhu who reigned at Anuradhapura about B.C. 80. An invasion of the Malabars from the continent forced him to fly from his throne and hide in the caves of Dambulla. After many years of concealment, he succeeded in regaining his throne, and greatfully embellished his rocky asylum. The statue of Vishnu in this chamber is held to be of peculiar sanctity ; and at the present day the ordeal by oath, and even by hot oil, is practised before it.*

The next temple, called the Mahá Viháre, or great temple, is by far the finest and largest of the five. It measures 160 feet by 50 ; and its greatest height is about 23 feet, the roof sloping downwards towards the back of the cave, where it is only four feet high. The first impression of the cave when the doors are opened is very striking : the coolness, the gloom, the

* The visitor who wishes to study the History of Buddhism, and its relations to Hinduism, is referred to Bishop Copleston's work on Buddhism, and the handbooks to Buddhism and Hinduism by Prof. Rhys Davids and Sir M. Monier Williams.

circle of sedent Buddhas dimly visible, and the death-like stillness, combine to produce a superstiticus feeling which the true believer translate into reverence. Note the roof paintings ; in the centre, Buddha in glory, worshipped by gods ; to the left, Buddha assaulted by the powers of evil. There are 53 statues in all, most of them exceeding life-size. On the left of the entrance is a well-proportioned dágoba, surrounded by sedent Buddhas, some of which have a canopy formed by the hooded cobra. Past the dágoba to the left there is a large statue of King Walagam Báhu, who is said to have begun this great shrine ; and facing it, on the roof, are depicted Buddha's wars with demons, the story of his life, and the worship, paid him by various divinities. Opposite to the King, among some curtains, is an upright figure of Buddha and canopy, both cut from the solid rock. There are some curious frescoes at the back of the line of statues that face the entrance ; first come three Hindu divinities, Gana or Ganesha, Kattragam and Wibhishana ; then a long procession of Rahat (Illuminati) priests ; then a painting of King Dutu-gemunu and his relations ; and close to it, the great combat between that monarch and the Malabar usurper, Eláļa. The latter has just received his death-wound from the king's javelin, and is being held on his elephant by an attendant. The swords in the hands of the fighting men are exactly similar to that dug up in the bund of Kaláwewa tank,* though widely different from the Sinhalese sword of the present day. At the eastern extremity of the cave there is a small recess covered with historical paintings. The landing of Wijeya—an outlawed prince from India—who is said to have arrived in Ceylon with a·

* See Part II., chap. 4.

few followers in B.C. 543, conquered the aborigines, (the picture which represents the queen on her war horse cutting off the aborigines' heads is curious), and established the Sihnalese in the Island,—the planting of the Bó tree at Anuradhapura, the dedication of relics to the Ruwanweli dágoba at the same place, and of the island to Buddha, figured by a king guiding an elephant-plough, are represented on the walls with more attention to history than proportion ; as the fish in the ocean which Wijeya is crossing are considerably larger than the vessel which carries him, and the heads of the worshippers at the dágoba overtop the building, which in reality is more than 200 feet high.   Not far from this recess, on the southern side of the cave, is a large wooden statue of Rája Kirti Sri Nissanga, to whom the shrine owes most of its glories, and near it is a huge modern image of the recumbent Buddha.   Opposite this statue, and towards the middle of the cave, is a small stone enclosure, containing a vessel which catches water that drips from a fissure in the roof. The fissure is ornamented with paintings of fish and the water is used for temple purposes.

The remaining chambers are by no means so interesting or imposing as the two first.   The third is known as the ' Maha Alut Wihára ' or great new wihára, and is 78 feet long, and from 30 to 60 feet broad.   There are 54 statues altogether in this chamber, including a large reclining figure of Buddha near the western wall, built of brick and about 30 feet long ; and near the northern wall, a wooden statue of Rája Kirti Sri Nissanga, with a curious stone sedent Buddha, unfinished, at its foot.   In the centre of the chamber, there is a large stone sedent Buddha under a stone canopy.

The fourth chamber or "Paspilime Wihára" is of smaller dimensions, being about 40 feet long by 30 broad. It contains several statues of Buddha, and a small dágoba with a copper top.   It is worth going into, if only to look at the wooden doorway to the right-hand side of the main entrance, which is covered with old and curious carving.

The fifth chamber is of very much the same size, but quite modern, having been constructed by a Kandyan chief in the early part of this century.   It contains a gigantic Buddha, about 35 feet long, and several smaller statues.

The Buddhist priests are directly forbidden by their creed to receive money : a prohibition which does not, it is feared, prevent their greedily demanding gratuities from strangers

CHAPTER II.

SIGIRI.

THE fortified rock of Sigiriya is so well worth a visit, especially now that the excavation of the ruins there is complete, that the visitor must not be deterred by what must be admitted to be the considerable difficulty of getting there. It lies $11\frac{1}{2}$ miles N.N.E. of Dambulla. The first two miles are along the metaled road that runs due North to Anuradhapura. There the metaled road to Trincomalee branches off to the East; and after going down that road for four miles, the visitor arrives at a small hamlet called Inamaluwa, just beyond which a jungle road to the right turns off to Sigiriya, which is five miles and a half away to the N.N.E. The metaled roads are always in excellent order, but the same cannot be said of the jungle road, which in dry weather is heavy with sand, and in wet weather with mud. The easiest way of doing the journey is on a bicycle (which can be conveyed by coach to Dambulla). It is usually possible to bicycle along about two-thirds of the jungle road, and thus the whole journey takes under two hours. Failing a bicycle, it is best to try and hire a bullock-cart or hackery at Dambulla to take one as far as Inamaluwa, whence the walk to Sígiriya and back, being mostly in the shade of the forest, is by no means impossible.   Or a carriage and pair can be hired at Mátale to go as far as Inamaluwa (but this is a costly proceeding : for terms apply to the Rest-house-keeper, Mátale).   There remain the two alterna-tives of walking all the way—possible but very fatiguing—and of going on horseback—the best way of all, but in-volving the possession of horses, as none are hireable at at Mátale or Dambulla.

There is a small resthouse at Sígiriya, where food and accommodation can be got, on notice being given before-hand.   The pleasantest time of year to make the expedi-tion is from the middle of January to the middle of March. July and August are to be avoided owing to the high wind then prevailing.   In very dry weather, ticks are unpleasantly numerous ; but they can be more or less guarded against by wearing high boots and by the use of strong carbolic soap.

The curious cylindrical rock rises abruptly from the plain to a height of about 400 feet, and the traveller will get a good view of it about a quarter of a mile be-fore reaching the resthouse.   From the resthouse he will proceed to the foot of the bund, which he will notice is out of all proportion to the small tank below, and marks the remains of a far more important irrigation work.   Following the narrow track along the bund, he will reach at the other end of the steep path that leads up to the large main terrace below the rock.   (The way is not difficult to find, but it is just as well to secure a village-guide at the resthouse.)

He should then work round below the rock from S. to N. till he comes to the stone cistern (commonly known as the King's Bath), whence he will get a fine view of the recent excavations along the lower W. face of the rock, showing the two stairways by which access was obtained to the rock gallery that led round the rock to the palace on the summit. Above this gallery he will see the very curious and unique "gallery of frescoes," a descripton of which is given later. Several of the figures can be plainly seen, and a preliminary idea obtained of the natural difficulties which the artist had to contend with.

Of the two staircases leading down from the rock gallery, Mr. Bell says :—

"Working from the Rock scarp a few yards south of the existing ascent into the ' gallery ' at the wide grooves which once held the ' gallery ' walls, the parties very soon struck two sets of stairs (*quartz* here again) branching off south-west and north-west and descending by a series of level landings and flights of steps. These stairs have been slowly followed—each with its flanking brick wall to the right of the ascent—down to the terrace immediately above the ' Audience Hall ' and ' Cistern ' rocks.

" The southern descent manifestly runs along the slope of a south-westerly spur of the Great Rock, and finally curls inwards at the bottom, fully 10 ft. below present ground level.

" That on the north—six flights of steps at least, with intermediate landings – mounts straight up due east from the ground just outside a stone gateway a little north-east of the ' Audience Hall,' until, nearing the Rock, it con-

verges to the south-east, and probably met the termination of the south approach at the ' gallery.'

" Some of these quartz staircases had as many as
twenty to thirty steps, beautifully dressed and several are
still in excellent preservation."

The visitor should descend to his left below the
" Cistern " rock, and inspect the magnificent rock-cut
" Audience Hall" and the smaller stone throne at its foot.
Notice the round stone at the back of this throne, where
possibly the umbrella-bearer stood.   Amid the stillness of
the jungle and the absolute desolation of the spot, it is
curious to picture the bright pageants and stately ceremonies that once enlivened this striking place of assembly.
To the left of the " Audience `Hall," and immediately
under the " Cistern," is a curious shrine with a stone
pedestal where stood a statue of Buddha ; and on the
roof overhead are remains of the old fresco painting and
plaster. Opposite the foot of the Audience Hall is a
well-cut stone seat

Ascending again to the " Cistern," the visitor should
push Northwards between some boulders, up a staircase,
and along the forest ; gradually mounting to the N.W.
corner of the upper platform, and so to the excavated
rooms on that platform. These rooms were all built on
the outer edge of the enclosure ; the windows no doubt
facing inwards towards the paved courtyard. He will
then see the flight of steps leading up towards the
(modern) iron ladders, and on either side of these steps
will observe three claws and the dew-claw of the gigantic
lion which evidently formed the marvel and the epony-
mous feature of the fortress (Sígiri=Siṇha giri, lion rock).

Until Mr. Bell unearthed these claws in 1898, there was nothing to show how the rock came by its name. Notice also to the left, high upon the rock, the huge hives of the "Bambara" bees, whose aggressive tendencies were a serious nuisance to the coolies when work began here in 1895, and necessited an organised attack with fire balls on the principal hive; since which disastrous day they have relinquished opposition and acquiesced in the British occupation.

The ascent of the rock is very easy, by means of the stout iron ladders and hand rails now provided. It was a very different matter previously to 1894, when the ladders were only jungle sticks tied with jungle rope, and the rest of the climb had to be accomplished by clinging on with fingers and toes to the grooves in the rock. These grooves, of course, formed the stepping for the wall that protected the final approach to the summit.

Mr. Bell gives the following description of the very interesting excavations on the summit :—

"Directly in front, looking south from the vantage ground of the east to west cross bank, stretched below as far as the central *pokuṇa*, is so much of the lower area as lies between the Rock's north and east edges and the high ridge that occupies the western half of the summit. Most here is comparatively level—the only level portion of any extent in a citadel where terraced arrangement was inevitable from the irregular conformation of the Rock's surface. This area was seemingly allotted to courtyards, passages, and side rooms. Half-way a winding staircase of three or four flights of steps—the longest on the Rock, and pierced at its head through tall flanking walls—shows the means of direct communication with the upper area to the west. At the side of these stairs is the magnificently carved '*gal-âsanaya*,' or granite throne, discovered in 1895.

" On the left, skirting the east edge of the Rock, was a range of minor rooms and passages, doubtless communicating with an outermost corridor, which almost encircled the citadel. This series of side chambers was continued on to near the south end of the Rock, interrupted only at the pond, where extra rooms, &c., intervene.

" As I had occasion to note in last year's Report :—

"That part of the ancient citadel lying south of the pond, and east of the high-level strip, was laid out in a series of cross-terraces, east and west, varying in width—and falling away southwards. From the *pokuna* to the foot of the last staircase at the extreme south are seven or eight distinct terraces...... The centre is taken up with an open courtyard and passages leading to the pond, and round it, on either side, by stairs and intermediate landings—all admirably planned to suit the physical conditions, and displaying great ingenuity in turning to full account the limited space and surface inequalities of the Rock's summit.*

" More than one of these terraces has been curtailed and hideously disfigured by *single-brick walls* of later construction—' patched up into a smoothless and smugness ' Ruskin forcibly pronounces ' more tragic than uttermost ruin.'

" The lowest staircase—at the south-west corner of

* C.A.S. Journal, vol. XIV., No. 47, 1896, p. 251.

the Rock—descends with a right angle return to the 'watch-cave' in the perpendicular crag on this side. The southernmost terrace, to the east of these stairs, was clearly dedicated to Cloacina.

"Of the higher level half of the summit I have already spoken, as containing a succession of apartments, rising in tiers northwards.

"The back bone, as it were, of the citadel is found in the paved way, with steps descending ever and anon, that was carried along its axis from end to end, hugging the retaining wall of the upper ridge, and winding with its angles, but for the most part running straight as an arrow. From this 'spinal column' branch off, east and west, staircase 'ribs,' which would render communication between all parts of the citadel easy and rapid; whilst each section was equally well served, by the cunningly designed interconnection of its own component divisions, through a maze of minor passages and stairs.

"No less perfectly planned was the *water supply*. The rock-hewn *pokuṇa*, nearly 30 yards square, centrally situated and accessible from every side, would suffice, when replenished yearly by the north-east monsoon rains, for ordinary requirements during the ensuing dry months. For drinking water resort was had, in all probability, to two at least of the three smaller cisterns close to the Rock's north, south-west, and south-east edges.

"A word or two regarding the *architectural construction* of the citadel.

"Further lengthening of the deep longitudinal trench, begun last year from the extreme southern verge, confirms the impressions that the foundations were throughout the low-level area, in general, of that form of stonework known as 'irregular horizontal,' and run down to the rock core. Upon this rested brick walls, vertical or in batter, plain or moulded, according to position and purpose, but all alike coated thickly with a tough plaster, white and polished, that has resisted the damp in places to this day. The massiveness of many of these walls bespeaks considerable height originally, despite the fact that the brickwork was almost dry-laid and indifferently bonded crosswise. But in 'make' these ancient bricks —some a cubit in length—shame most of our modern outturn, being as well burnt as they are sharp and close.

" Of the systém of *roofing* we know nothing beyond the certainty that it was timbered throughout and flat-tiled, in the style familiar among the Anurádhapura ruins.

" A marked feature of the ground plan is the *erratic location of steps*. As often as not, they are pushed aside from the centre of the rooms into which they lead, and relegated to all sorts of odd corners. This vagary was no doubt forced upon the architects by the unconformable surface of the rock, which had to be reckoned with everywhere.

" But noteworthy, above all, is the *complete absence of monolith pillars and stone-carved doorways*, the most salient characteristic of ancient structures in the Island. Whilst quartzous steps and flagstones were livishly employed to enhance the beauty of this peerless citadel, not one fragment of column, door-frame, or window-sash in *stone* has come to light on *Sigiri-gala*. Above the floor all was of brick or wood. As for gneiss,

with the sole exception of the noble throne above men.
tioned—like silver in the days of Solomon—'it was
nothing accounted of,' and finds no place in Kásyapa's
citadel."

Descending by the way he came, the visitor should
strike up towards what is left of the great gallery by the
Northern approach. This flight of steps is incomplete,
and he must cross over to the Southern flight, which will
lead him to the transit of rock grooves, ending in the iron
ladder which lands him on the gallery floor. It is un-
necessary to expatiate on the skill and boldness of this
engineering marvel: it forms a very striking commentary
upon an epoch and a civilisation of which we are lamentab-
ly ignorant; and we are as puzzled to account for the conception as for the execution of such a weird undertaking.
The plaster on the high retaining wall is still as smooth
and brilliant as on the day when it was applied; and
some of the names and inscriptions that are scribbled on
it have at least the excuse of dating back to the age of
the original builders.

High above this gallery is the famous picture gallery,
justly considered inaccessible until, in 1889, Sir A. Gordon
determined to have the frescoes copied, and entrusted
the task to the competent hands of Mr. A. Murray,
P.W.D. This is Mr. Murray's account of his successful
attempt to reach the gallery :—

" Holes were jumped into the rock face, one above the
other, as the timber staging was carried up, and iron
jumpers driven home and secured with cement. To these
the staging was lashed and rendered secure. Once the
chamber was reached a hemp rope ladder with wooden
rungs was made fast to stout iron stanchions sunk into
the floor of the chamber itself and made as rigid as possi-

ble by attachment to the staging. The erection of the staging was by no means an easy matter............ It was found that the floor of the 'pocket' was at too steep an angle to admit of any one sitting, much less standing. Iron stanchions were therefore let into the floor, and a strong trestle, or framework, made secure to them. On this was placed a platform, from which the work of copying the frescoes was carried out. The frescoes being painted on the roof and upper sections of the sides of the chamber, the staging, as erected, made it only possible to copy them by lying at full length on back or side."

Mr. Murray securied copies in coloured chalks of 13 out of the 17 frescoes ; but it remained for Mr. Bell, and his talented draughtsman, Mr. Perera, to obtain, in 1896-97, facsimile oil paintings of all the frescoes, and also to paint the caves from midair. This daring feat was accomplished as follows :—

" A 4-in. hawser was lowered to the ground from the summit over the west clift (which here projects considerably), and a strong iron block bound to the end. Through this block a 2-in. rope was passed, and an improvised chair firmly tied on to it: the hawser was then pulled half way up the Rock scarp. Hauled up thus, one swung in the air upwards of 150 ft. above the ground, and 50 ft. clear of the cliff.

" Instantaneous photographs were tried, but with little success, owing to the strong wind and an indifferent drop-shutter.

" On the other hand, after a week's ' rocking ' in space, Mr. Perera completed an excellent little oil painting, to scale (about $\frac{1}{32}$nd).   This shows at a glance the re-lative position of the several figures."

Of the the frescoes themselves, Mr. Bell says :—

"Only three pigments were used, *yellow, red*, and *green*, though *black* seems to have been given a trial as back-ground to one figure, No. 14 ' B.'   The particular shades of these colours predominating the paintings may best be realized from the modern corresponding media employed by Mr. Perera in copying them, viz., chrome yellow yellow ochre, raw sienna, burnt sienna, raw umber, light red, Indi-an red, sap green, terra vert, lamp black, and flake white.

" The entire omission of *blue* is very remarkable, and difficult to account for, as this colour enters freely into the sister paintings at Ajanṭa.

"The scene intended to be pourtrayed would seem to be *a procession of the queens and princesses* of Kásyapa's court, with their attendants, on the way to worship at the Buddhist viháré at *Pidurá-gala*, the hill lying about a mile north of Sígiriya.   The figures are manifestly all moving in that direction, and the flowers held in their hands by the ladies, and carried after them by servant-maids, can hardly bear any other signification.   Grouping in pairs is chiefly favoured throughout : usually queen or princess followed by a lady-in-waiting of the same, or kindred, blood, or by a dark-skinned maidservant of alien race.   The latter (Nos. 4, 8, 11 of ' B') are given a greenish complexion—a ' badge of servitude' which clearly marks them off from the high-born dames, their mistresses, whether pale-yellow ' blondes ' or orange-hued ' brunettes '-—all three coloured types reproduced frequently at Ajanṭa.

"The type of features is Aryan—oval face, thick fleshy lips, but straight, almost Grecian nose and forehead. The 'almond-eyes' of No. 1 'B' betoken a slight tinge of Mongolian blood."

If the visitor has time in hand, he may with advantage explore the many curious rocks lying in the vicinity of the main rock, where he will find frequent and interesting remains of the old life :—cave-dwellings, steppings innumerable for walls, pieces of fresco, and outer lines of defence : and he should particularly inspect the very remarkable "Preaching Rock," lying E.N.E. of Sigirigala with its triple pulpit and intricate wall-lines.

CHAPTER III.

ANURADHAPURA.

NURADHAPURA (Post and Telegraph Office) is the capital of the North-Central Province —the second largest province in Ceylon, having an area of 4,046 square miles. This province was created by Governor Sir William Gregory in 1873, it having formerly been an appendage of the Northern Province. Its first administrator was the Hon. Sir J. F. Dickson, K.C.M.G.; afterwards Colonial Secretary of the Straits Settlements. It has a scattered population of 75,333, the large majority of whom are Sinhalese, though the Tamils are rapidly on the increase; and the cultivation of paddy is the almost universal occupation of both races. The town is situated on a level plain at an elevation of 312 feet above the sea, and has a present population of about 2,508, comprising a large number of Moormen, who are the chief " boutique-keepers " and traders of the place. The average mean temperature for the last 10 years is 80·1; the hottest months being March and April: while the annual rains extend from October to the end of the year. The average annual rainfall is 51·66 inches. It is the headquarters of the only two Revenue Officers in the Province—the Government Agent and Assistant Government Agent; who also combine judicial duties. The amount of new land which, thanks to an enlightened irrigation policy, is being cleared and planted on all sides in the neighbourhood of the town, will strike the most casual observer.

The horse-coach, carrying passengers and mails to Anuradhapura, leaves Dambulla at 12-30 p.m. (The table of fares will be found at the end of the book). The distance to Anuradhapura, which is reached at 6 p.m., is 42 miles, viz., 14 to Kekirawa, 14 to Tirappane (at both which places there are excellent resthouses), and 14 to the terminus. The Anuradhapura resthouse is newly-built and decidedly comfortable and well-found. During the tourist season, a telegram with reply prepaid, enquiring whether a room is available, is by far the wiser course, as the accommodation is limited, and the influx of travellers considerable.

A guide can be procured at the resthouse, and also a spring bullock-cart and pair of bulls, or a horse and carriage, at rates fixed by the Government Agent.

It may be as well to point out here that the following description of the ruins is rather popular than exhaustive and scientific; and that the traveller who has time to spare and wishes to make study of the subject, cannot do better than purchase the seven Archæological Reports brought out by Mr. H. C. P. Bell (Archæological Commissioner,) which are furnished with admirable plans and diagrams, and can be purchased at a most reasonable price from the Government Record Office, Colombo.

The visitor may conveniently begin operations by inspecting the so-called Brazen Palace, which is a vast collection of monolithic granite pillars 1,600 in number, standing about 12 feet out of the ground, and arranged in lines of 40 each way. They cover a space measuring 231 feet 2 inches from North to South, and 232 feet 2 inches from East to West. The pillars are rough and undressed (the corner pillars being more than double the size of the rest) and retain the marks of the wedges by which they were split off in the quarry: they were probably coated with chunam, and perhaps covered with copper. They formed the foundations of the Lówámaha-páya or Great Brazen Palace, erected by King Dutu-gemunu in the 2nd century B.C., and supported a building nine stories in height, containing 1,000 dormitories for priests and other apartments. The roof of this vast monastery was of sheet copper: the walls, says the native chronicle, were embellished with beads resplendent like gems, the great hall was supported on golden pillars resting on lions; in the centre was an ivory throne, with a golden sun and a silver moon on either side; and above all glittered the imperial " Chatta," the white canopy of dominion. The monastery was reconstructed, and reduced to 7 stories in height, in B.C. 140; and in A. D. 301 was pulled down by the apostate Rája, Maha Sen; but penitently restored by him on his recantation. Its last restoration took place in the reign of King Prákrama Báhu, towards the close of the twelfth century.

At the South-Eastern corner of the Brazen Palace is a collection of huge monolithic capitals, carved with most grotesque designs, of which the visitor will be reminded when he goes to Isurumuniya. On the opposite side of the Sacred Road which passes the Palace, is an oblong enclosure with a plain entablature and a few detached pillars; this is known as the Ransimálakaya or private hall, and is said to have been used for confessional purposes by the priests before they entered the Brazen Palace. The basement of this building was excavated and restored by the Royal Asiatic Society, 1895-6.

Proceeding Southwards for a short distance down the Sacred Road—the track along which the pilgrims come, and have come for 2,000 years, to offer their devotions to the most venerated symbols of their religion,—the visitor reaches the enclosure which surrounds the celebrated Bó-tree. This tree (*ficus religiosa*) is the oldest historical tree in the world. It was planted 245 years before Christ, and is therefore now 2,130 years old. The story of its arrival is a curiously early instance of that hardly-used modern term—Women's Rights. The royal missionary Mahindo* had converted the Rája and people of Anuradhapura to the tenets of pure Buddhism with miraculous rapidity; and the effects of his zealous preaching were by no means confined to the male sex. Queen Anula and thousands of her country-women became earnest followers of the new cult; and begged to be allowed to take the vows of self-devotion. These vows, however, Mahindo declared himself unable to administer to their sex; and suggested that his sister Sanghamitta, an abbess in India, should be sent for to admit the novices. She responded to the call; and with her, the King of Pattilipatta (the modern Patna) sent a branch of the Sacred Bó-tree under which Gautama sat on the day that he attained to Buddha-hood.

The story of this tree's life has been handed down in a continuous series of authentic chronicles. It was care-

* See the chapter on Mihintale.

fully tended, enriched with stone-carvings and terraces,
and honoured with magnificent ceremonies, by successive
dynasties : and was spared amid the havoc of invasions,
owing its immunity either to divine protection, to superstitious reverence, or to its intrinsic worthlessness to a
plunderer. It was visited by the Chinese traveller, Fa
Hian, in the fifth century A.D., and was endowed with
lands by Rája Sinha, the despot of Kandy, so late as
A.D. 1739.

The entrance into the grove of palms and bó-trees
which surrounds the Sacred Tree is worth studying.
Notice on either side of the chief gateway the palm tree
growing out of the centre of a bó-tree, which is by some
supposed to be a remnant of phallic worship. The semi-
circular stone at the foot of the steps is a good specimen
of a " moonstone." These stones are found in other
parts of the ruins ; the main design is the same in all ; but
not one is precisely the same, either in arrangement or
detail. As a general rule, the outer border of the stone
presents a procession of the elephant, the horse, the lion
and the Brahmany bull ; the next two or three circles
show designs taken from the stem and leaf of the lotus
plant ; then comes a procession of the " hanza," or sacred
goose ; and the innermost circles represent the other
stages of the lotus growth—the flower, and the round bud.
The two rounded stones at the lower termination of the
balustrade represent door guardians (dvarpal). The pattern is common with slight variations throughout the
ruins ; the figures are always in high relief, and generally
have grotesque supporters at their feet. The upper portion
of the balustrade is formed of the head, and trunk of a
fabulous and quaint animal—half-crocodile, half-elephant

—which is also an emblem common to all the ruined stairways. Entering the grove, there is a large stone image of Buddha to the right, and several images to the left, all more or less dilapidated. In the Southern part of the grove are eight recumbent pillars (monoliths) of excellent workmanship. The Sacred Tree itself—a straggling and feeble specimen compared to some of its congeners in the grove—is surrounded by three tiers of terraces. On the Eastern side of the first terrace is a ruined brick sedent figure of Buddha. The main approach to the second terrace is on the West side, the arch of the doorway being surmounted by a "Makara Torana." The leaves which fall from the Sacred Tree are highly esteemed as relics by the thousands of pilgrims who come to worship it during the full moons of June and July.

A little to the South of the Sacred Bó-tree, on the right-hand side of the Kurunégala road, there is a circle of very fine monolithic pillars with elaborate capitals, surrounding a low mound. These mark the site of a sacred building—a Vihára—miscalled the Mayurapáya, or Peacock Palace, built in the first century of the Christian era, and popularly said to be so named from the luxuriance of the precious stones and metals that adorned it. Still further south, on the same side, is a huge mound which marks the tomb of Eláḷa.*   Nearly opposite to the Peacock Palace is the Government Civil Hospital.

Proceeding Northwards from the Bó-tree down the Sacred Road, the visitor passes on his left a ruin known as the "Adáhaná Sáláwa," or place of cremation of the Kings; and soon after, on his right, a somewhat similar ruin, popularly called the "Wirawitta Sáláwa," or place

* See part I., p. 6.

of lamentation for the Royal Family. Near this are three recumbent stone bulls, of various sizes and great antiquity. Sinhalese women believe that by turning one of these completely round, they will avert barrenness. One of these bulls, apparently, used formerly to revolve on a pivot,* a sensible aid towards the fulfilment of the mystic rite. Further up the road, there is a curious stone sarcophagus, said by tradition to have been King Duṭugẹmunu's medicine bath, and measuring 7 ft. 2 in. long by 2 ft. 6 in. wide : and beyond, is an enclosure of small square pillars surrounding a large raised slab of granite, said to have been the couch on which Duṭugẹmunu passed his last hours, within view of his proudest monument—the Ruwaṇvẹli. At the back of this enclosure, there is a large Mûtragala of exquisite workmanship.

Immediately opposite to this slab, is the main entrance to the Ruwaṇvẹli (golden-dust) dágoba. This was begun by King Duṭugẹmunu, about B.C. 161, partly to celebrate his victory over the Tamil usurper Elaḷa,† partly from a superstitious desire to carry out an ancient prophecy. It was completed by his successor, Saddhá Tissa, in B.C. 140. Its original outline was destroyed by the Malabars, A.D. 1214. Its present height is about 150 feet, with a diameter of 379 feet. It is now being restored by the pious contributions of pilgrims, and the zealous efforts of the Chief Priest. Passing through the principal gateway (called " mura-gé," or guard-house, and lately restored), the visitor should turn to the right for a few yards and look at the curious circular " pokuna" (bathing place), the only one of its kind in the ruins. It measures 60 feet

* Forbes' Eleven Years in Ceylon, 2nd ed., Vol. 1., p. 213.
† See part I.

in diameter at the surface, by 25 feet deep; and the gradually concentrating layers of granite blocks are still very perfect.   Returning to the main approach, he comes to a second (ruined) "mura-gé"; and to the right of its stairway will see two large stone lotus plants.   There is a fine frieze of lions running along the upper border of the platform.

The dágoba was originally surrounded by two large paved courts or platforms, the inner one raised above the outer.   Round the outer side of the inner boundary wall there was originally a complete circle of elephants, made out of brickwork, and coated with chunam : each elephant being furnished, says the Mahawaṇso, with tusks of real ivory.   Most of these figures have fallen away beyond recognition ; but in some few the shape of the animal is still plainly discernible.   Near the N.E. angle of the outer enclosure is a huge octangular granite pillar —the largest monolith in the ruins—which is said to have been removed by King Duṭugẹmunu from the centre of the area now covered by the Ruwaṇvẹli, and to have borne an ancient inscription and prophecy, that on this spot a superb dágoba should be raised by a pious and fortunate monarch, which attracted the superstition of the King.   There is a small "viháre" or temple at the termination of the main Eastern approach, which contains nothing of interest except a small recumbent figure of Buddha brought by devotees from Siam.   Round the outside of the " viháre," near the ground, runs a remark. able frieze of grotesque figures in high relief.   Proceeding to the left, round the base of the dágoba, there are five large upright statues and a small sedẹnt one ; the latter still bearing traces of the gilding which once covered it.

The tallest statue is said to be of King Duṭugęmunu.
Further on is a statue in the attitude of adoration, facing
the dágoba which is said to represent King Bhátiya Tisa,
who reigned at the dawning of the Christian era, and was
the only layman ever permitted to enter the underground
passage and explore the wonders of the inner treasure-
chamber of the Ruwaŋvęli.*   The entrance to this
passage is said to be marked by a small pit and mound,
with stone ruins, about 60 yards to the south of the outer
boundary wall.   The small granite dágoba near Bhátiya
Tisa's statue is said to have been made as a model for the
larger structure.   There is a large stone altar on the
N.,S.,E., and W. sides of the dágoba, that to the west
being the most perfect ; and several smaller altars and
broken statues.   Many traces of the gaudy painting which
formerly adorned (or disfigured) these altars may still be
seen ; and it should be remembered that the whole dágoba
was originally pure white, being incrusted with a preparation of lime, coconut water, and the glutinous juice
of the " Para " tree (*dillena dentata*), and taking a polish
nearly equal to marble.

The description of the building of this dágoba takes
up a great deal of the early part of the Mahawaŋso.   It
is particularly noted that, as an extra mark of piety, the
labour employed upon it was paid for ; moreover, as the
people were too poor, after the Tamil wars, to make the
enormous quantity of bricks required, heaven came to
the pious monarch's aid, and, at Sakra's orders, the god

---

* Sir E. Tennent notices the resemblance between this story
and that of the descent of Daniel and King Astyage, into the
temple of Bel, by the privy entrance under the table whereby
the priests entered ŕ 'd consumed the offerings made to the idol.—
(Bel and the Dragoŋ Apoch, ch. 1-12.)

Wismakarma made them in a night at a spot 16 miles distant, and then, taking the form of a lizard, pointed them out in the morning to a Veddá, or aborigine,* who was out there shooting with his dogs, and hastened to inform the King of the miracle.

Leaving the Ruwaṇvẹli by the western entrance, the visitor should explore the green park which stretches northwards towards the Thúpáráma dágoba. The park is thickly studded with ruins; some of them having probably been the residences of priests connected with the two neighbouring dágobas. Many of the pillars and flights of steps are well worthy of minute inspection.

Immediately to the S.E. of the Thúpáráma are the remains of a large oblong enclosure known as the Daladá Máligáwa, or Palace of the Tooth. This can be easily recognized by the unique cuneiform mouldings of the capitals of the pillars. This building was erected by King Kírti Sri Megahawarna, in A.D. 311, to receive the Sacred Tooth (Daladá) of Buddha, which was brought over from India in charge of a princess of Káliṇga, who concealed it in the folds of her hair; and here it was seen by the Chinese traveller, Fa Hien, about 413 A.D., who minutely describes the ceremonies and processions which accompanied its exhibition to the pious. It is supposed that the moulding on the pillars is meant to represent the sacred relic. The Thúpáráma is the oldest of the great dágobas of Anuradhapura, and the most venerated dágoba in Ceylon. It was built by King Dewánaṇpiya Tisa in B.C. 307 to

* It is noticeable that the term used to describe the Veddá is honorific. Perhaps the position of the Saxons in England during the reign of Richard I. may have been analogous to that of the Veddás in Ceylon at this epoch.

enshrine the right collar-bone of Buddha. In A.D. 400 King Upatisa caused a case to be made for it, of metal ornamented with gold; and about fifty years ago a pious priest collected funds from the devout for clearing it of jungle and coating it with chunam, though his dubious restoration is more likely to gain for him the admiration of the devotee than the gratitude of the archæologist. Its height is 63 feet; it is surrounded by three rows of graceful pillars, with 52, 36, and 40 pillars in each row respectively; all the shafts being monoliths. Fergusson, in his Handbook to Architecture (Vol. I., p. 41), pronounces this dágoba to be "older than any monument now existing on the continent of India."

Fifty yards to the east of the Thúpáráma, on the north side of the inner circular road, is a beautifully carved cistern, 10 ft long by 5 ft. 3 in. wide and 2 ft. 6 in. deep, made out of a single block of granite, and said to date from the time of Duṭugęmunu. It was probably used to hold food for the priests; and only three years ago, two korales (or shires) subscribed to fill it with food for the pilgrims of the June full moon. Close to this cistern has now been placed a curious stone known as a " panduorua," or dyeing-vessel. It is oblong in shape, and has a deep circular hollow at one end, and a small raised platform at the other. This stone was used exclusively for the dyeing of priests' robes: the yellow "pandu," or dye (formed by boiling various vegetable ingredients) was poured into the hollow, the robes soaked in it, and then laid on the platform in order that the dye might be thoroughly worked into them by means of wooden rollers. The shady road running northwards from the Thúpáráma leads to the Jétawanáráma, and so to the outer circular road; but the visitor will probably make a second expedition to this road.

He will therefore continue on by the inner circular road, passing Baswakkulam tank on his right, and soon after, on his left, the residence of the Assistant Government Agent, that of the Government Agent, and the Kachcheri. He can obtain leave from the Government Agent to go into his office in the Kachcheri, where will be found a miscellaneous collection of earthenware, large copper vessels, glazed tiles, ironwork, etc., dug up in the neighbourhood ; while in the Kachcheri compound he will see various ancient inscriptions, images, "mûtragal " (urinal stones), and other stone work.

If the visitor is pressed for time he is recommended to omit the first three miles of the outer circular drive, and, instead, to make straight for the Thúpáráma, and from that up the road to the Lankáráma Dágoba (see p., 55 and so to the outer circular at the third mile post ; and thence along that road as described on p. 55. He will thus see all the important sights of the outer circular by the quickest route. But if he has time to make the complete circuit— and the drive is very attractive—he will start from the Post Office, and passing on the left the entrance to the Experi-mental Gardens, (which are quite worth a visit) and on the right the Jail (which is built to hold 70 prisoners), the visitor will see on his right the Miriswetiya dágoba. This was erected about the middle of the second century B.C. by King Duṭugẹmunu. The reason for its erection gives a curious insight into the character of the pious Rája. He remembered one day that he had on a certain occasion partaken of a common accompaniment of curry known as " sambal " (weṭiya), and made partly of chillies (miris), without offering a share to a priest. Remorsefully anxious to expiate the omission, he was prompted by a miracle to build a great shrine in honor of Buddha, and to call it Miriswețiya, after the viand which had necessitated the atonement.

The chapel on the western side was excavated some years ago, and is a beautiful specimen of Sinhalese architecture. The ruined brickwork on the top of the chapel probably formed a niche for some image or relic. The other sides of the dágoba were partially excavated by the Royal Asiatic Society, and the whole dágoba is at the present time being elaborately restored at the expense of a Siamese prince. There are the remains of several shrines and buildings on all sides of the dágoba; the most notable being the collection of sixty-two enormous pillars (thirty-seven of which are still nearly perfect), about 80 yards to the west, which were probably the foundations of the residence of the college of priests attached to the service of the shrine.

The road next leads on to the bund of Tisávęwa; the road to the left leads round the bund from west to east. This makes a most pleasant walk, as there is nearly always a breeze, and the ripple of the water against the "rala-pana," or "wave catch" is very attractive. The visitor will find himself, after about a mile's walk, close to the Isurumuniya temple,(for which see p. 80) and can return by the Kurunégala road. Tisávęwa (vęwa=tank) was constructed by King Dewenipiatissa about 300 B.C., and is over three miles in circumference. It was restored in 1878, and is now largely utilised in the cultivation of the surrounding paddy-fields.* The outer cirular road,

* The following figures show that the restoration of the three large tanks in the immediate vicinity of Anuradhapura has had some effect upon the rice supply of the country.

	a.	r.	p.
(i) TISAVEWA.			
Extent cultivated before restoration	5	0	0
Extent opened up since restoration	910	2	17

(Continued on next page.)

properly so called, starts from the west of the spill, beyond the bridge, so as to avoid the ancient water-course known as the Yóda-ela or giant's channel : the first mile is devoid óf ruins, but is an extremely pretty drive, through low jungle fringed with handsome trees ; hares and deer occasionally dart across the path, and troops of monkeys chatter in the branches. Soon after the second mile-stone, on the left of the road, occurs the first of the (so-called) pavilions. Very little is really known about this, and the four similar buildings between the first and second mile-stones. They are all alike in design, varying only in size and minor details. Each of them has a main entrance facing the east, opening on to a low boundary wall about six feet wide, from which small flights of steps, at the middle of the N. and S. sides, lead into the inner enclosure. Each pavilion consists of two square platforms, of nearly equal dimensions, raised about $2\frac{1}{2}$ feet from the ground level, the outside wall consisting of plain, oblong slabs of granite ; the two sections being connected by enormous slabs, or landing stones ; the largest of which weighs nearly 25 tons. In each case, the eastern platform has no sign of pillars, while the western platform has about 16 narrow columns. Each pavilion is furnished with a pokuna, or small bathing tank, and several annexes. It is presumed that the roof was of timber, as there are

(Note continued from page 53.)

	a.	r.	p.
(ii) BASAWAKKULAM.			
Extent cultivated before restoration	12	0	0
Extent opened up since restoration	238	1	2

	a.	r.	p.
(iii) NUWARAVEWA.			
Extent cultivated before restoration	109	0	0
Extent opened up since restoration	246	0	35

In addition to this may be added about 150 acres of new land under coconuts, plantains, etc.

no remains of stone rafters. The first pavilion small pokuna in the N.E. corner of the enclosure, with a very perfect stone-built chamber or dressing-room.

The second pavilion, a little further down the road, has a fine pokuna to the S.W., and the design of the house is exactly repeated in miniature in a small annexe to the north.

The third pavilion is much larger and more perfect than the two former. It has a fine pokuna to the S.W., and a small and finely-moulded pillar in the N.E. corner perhaps marks the site of a shrine. To the north there are two annexes, the most easterly of which is very curious and unique, and suggests the idea of a small Court-house or Audience Hall. Notice the hollow circular stone for grinding paddy outside the N.E. corner of the outer enclosure.

The fourth pavilion (1¾ mile) is on the right-hand side of the road, and of still larger proportions. The porch is very perfect. There is a large reservoir to the south ; and a pokuna, with three almost subterranean chambers, to the north. The two tall pillars flanking the connecting pediment have graceful semi-circular capitals. There are annexes to the N.,S., and E.

The fifth pavilon is on the left side of the road. The pond is again almost perfect, and some curious drainage pipes of stone are exposed to view. Opposite, there is a large and curious pokuna ,and the ruins of several buildings.

From the second to the third mile-stone there are no ruins. Directly after the third mile-stone, a road turning to the right leads to the Lankáráma Dágoba. The visitor will see a continuation of this road running northwards into the jungle ; and proceeding some 50 yards along it, will notice on his right a jungle-path, which will conduct him to two sets of cave-dwellings. The brickwork which enclosed them is gone, but the dimensions of each cell can easily be made out. An enormous flat slab, fifteen feet in length, lies at right angles to the first cell, with a long inscription on it.* On the summit of the rock at the second set of cells there are four low altars for the reception of flower-offerings ; plainly marking the site of some important image or relic.

Following the main road, the visitor passes on his left a high ruined mound popularly known as Duṭugẹmunu's tomb ; close to which there is a fine ruin standing on an embankment made of large slabs of stone. This is popularly known as the Queen's Palace, but was undoubtedly a vihára. A treble row of tall pillars crown the southern boundary. The flight of stone steps leading up to the principal buildings is in fair preservation. The moon-stone at the base is a good specimen ; each step is ornamented with a row of three quaint male figures ; and on either side of the landing stone at the top is a well-executed carving of a lion in high relief and in the conventional attitude. On the platform itself are twenty-four stone pillars. A little farther on is a collection of eighty pillars about seven feet high, arranged in rows of ten ; and twelve much taller ones in close proximity. These were probably the foundation pillars of the monastery attached to the shrine. At the back of them, there is a large " pokuna."

A little further down the road, to the right, there is a sedent Buddha, about five-and-a-half feet high, but

* See Müller's Ceylon Inscriptions, pp. 27, 73, 109.

very much mutilated ; and beyond this, on the same side (at the $3\frac{1}{2}$ mile-post) is a square " Mantragala " stone with nine square holes in its upper surface at regular intervals.

It is impossible at present to pronounce authoritatively as to the actual use and meaning of these curious stones. Formerly they were called "Yogi" stones, and were supposed to have been used by ascetics for purposes of mystic devotion and second sight. But this is rendered improbable by the positions in which some of them have been found, and by the fact that one at least, if not more, was covered by a heavy stone slab. It seems clear that these stones were always square, and always divided into either 9 or 25 partitions; that probably they were laid down within shrines, below the floor, and covered with a slab upon which rested the *âsanaya*, or pedestal, of the image, or other object of worship ; that they were talismans against demoniac influences; that the 9 and 25 divisions had various mystic and astrological significations.*

There is a similar stone to this, with twenty-five small squares in the compound of the Government Agent's residence ; a second near the reading-room and the stone bulls ; and a third at the new excavations near the stone canopy.

To the south-east of this stone, an enormous "pokuna" is visible, which is known as the Elephants' Bathing Tank.†   Nearly opposite, on the left-hand side of the road,

---

* See Mr. Bell's Seventh Report to Government, Appendix A.

† There is a tendency in local tradition to presume that everything particularly large was intended for and used by elephants—a hypothesis not supported by investigation.

is a beautiful stone canopy, restored in 1886. The square centre-piece is particularly perfect, and perhaps the finest specimen of moulding in the ruins. The upper surface of the centre-piece measures 6 ft. by 7 ft. 3 in., with an inside depth of moulding of about 1 ft. 7 in.; while the total weight must exceed five tons. Excavations have lately been carried on all round it, which resulted in the discovery of three "Sannas" or inscribed stones. The inscriptions are of the 10th centrury. Two of them are in excellent preservation; one is framed, and the other two have plain edges The slab with a framed inscription measures 6 ft. 8 in. by 3 ft. 8 in. inside the frame. The other two measure 9 ft. by 3 ft. 9 in. and 7 ft. 3 in. by 4 ft. 2 in. respectively.

An enormous limestone slab measuring 16 ft. 10 in. by 6 ft. 1 in. has been turned up near the third "Sannasa" and also a large number of pillars, stairways, and frag. ments of the canopy; some of which were found as deep as seven feet under ground. But the whole place has been terribly and wilfully destroyed; and it possibly is rendered more puzzling by the remains of a second, or even a third, restoration.

Shortly after this, the road leads past a large collection of ruins, the most noticeable among them being the three "stone canoes," as they are called, which were possibly used to contain the food provided for the priests at the King's expense. Two are monolithic, the larger of them measuring 16 ft. by 3 ft. 7 in. The third one, which has been restored in modern times, measures 62 ft. 9 in. by 4 ft. 4 in. There are traces of large buildings on every side and the ground is red with broken tiles and bricks.

In the jungle exactly opposite to the " stone canoes," some interesting discoveries have been made. There is a large sedent Buddha, about 300 yards from the road to the eastward, in very fair preservation, and about 7 feet high. To the right of, and about 100 yards from, this statue, is a large collection of pillars, which evidently formed a great central hall or temple, with three large annexes. Notice the beautiful stairway and landing stone which are at the entrance to the central hall. As everything here, steps, landing-stone, door-guardians, and pillars, is on the largest scale, it was no doubt an important place ; but has not yet been identified. From the sedent Buddha close to this temple, a path now leads to two other fine buildings, about 200 and 300 yards distant. The first is oblong in shape, with very large monolithic pillars, the capitals elaborately carved. Notice the kneeling-stone, or granite fald-stool, in the centre of the building. The second "vihare" differs in design : the platform is square ; and along two sides of it, from East to West, run three rows of very tall monolithic pillars, with decorated capitals, leaving a broad space down the centre. They evidently supported a pagoda, or dome-shaped roof. Some portions of a bold, panelled frieze, which apparently ran round the inner boundary of the platform, have been unearthed, and lie around. This is one of the most picturesque spots in the ruins ; the graceful pillars slope in all directions, the floor of the platform heaves and undulates as though from an earthquake shock, the " moonstone " and carved stairs are cracked and riven, huge slabs and moulded fragments lie about in wild confusion, and the colours of the dead and living jungle relieve the grey monotony of granite.

Near this place there is a low wall of large stones which has been traced for a great distance each way, and is thought to mark the great East and West street mentioned in the Mahawanso. Further on are the gigantic pillars which are supposed to be the remains of the elephant stables.* These are 2 ft. square, and stand 16 ft. from the ground; and are in good preservation.† Beyond these again is a collection of low foundation pillars, probably marking a building, connected with the adjoining " King's Palace," as it is called, a building very similar in design to the " Queen's Palace," and also undoubtedly a shrine. Here are to be seen the most perfect " moon stone " and flight of steps yet discovered. Having been buried for centuries, they are almost as pefect as when they were first put into position. It will be seen that each of the sacred geese carries in its bill the flower, bud and leaf of the lotus. Notice the quaint door-guardians at the head of the stairs, and the lions beyond : every detail of the mane, claws, etc., of the latter being delicately and incisively finished off.

At the N.E. corner of this " Palace," a jungle path leads to a large "pokuna," and close to it is an extraordinary square well. It is a good deal dilapidated, but its shape is still fairly perfect ; it is lined with huge slabs of granite, measuring about 11 ft. long 2 ft. broad and one foot thick while the mouth of the well itself measured about 17 ft. by 15 ft. The well has at present been excavated to a depth of about 30 ft. It is difficult to say what use was made of this great work. The Sinhalese were not wont to build wells of such dimensions, and it may possibly have

---

* See note, page 57.   † See Mahawanso, ch. xiv.

been a " bisókotua " or sluice connected with the adjoining " pokuna".   But no inlet or outlet channels have so far been discovered.

The road next takes a semi-circular curve round the Jétawanáráma Dágoba.   This enormous shrine was built by King Mahá Séná* about the close of the third century A.D., to mark his recantation of the errors of the Wytulian heresy, to which he had been a temporary convert.

The height of the dágoba, including pedestal and spire, is 249 feet, and its diameter 360 feet ; and the cubic contents of the dome of brickwork and the platform on which it stands, are said by Tennent to exceed 20 millions of cubic feet.   The same author remarks with reference to this dágoba :—"Even with the facilities which modern invention supplies for economising labour, the building of such a mass would at present occupy 500 bricklayers from 6 to 7 years, and would involve an expenditure of at least a million sterling.   The materials are sufficient to raise 8,000 houses, each with 20 feet frontage, and these would form 30 streets half a mile in length.   They would construct a town, the size of Ipswich or Coventry ; they would line an ordinary railway tunnel 20 miles long, or form a wall, one foot thick and 10 feet high, reaching from London to Edinburgh."   But only the " glory of outline " is left to the Jétawanáráma ; its four chapels have crumbled away almost beyond recognition, enormous trees have eaten into the brickwork to the very summit, and troops of the large grey " wanderoo " monkey are the only devotees who frequent the holy place.

* See part I., page 9.

The road to the right leads round south of the dágoba through several ruined buildings and a shady drive into the inner circular road close to the Thúpáráma. The main road turns to the left, and, soon after the fourth mile-stone, passes a colossal sedent figure of Buddha, 7 ft. 6 in. high, which is regarded with great reverence by the pilgrims. Opposite to this statue, a path has been cut northwards into the jungle, which leads to a magnificent "pokuna" or bathing-pond. It is similar in detail to the "Kuṭṭam pokuna," but is square instead of oblong; and the long flight of steps instead of standing out from, is let into, the side wall. The stone pipe which fed it rests on an upright slab on which is carved a very grotesque Falstaffian figure in high relief; and probably was connected by a channel with Basawakkulam tank. Near the "pokuna" a very curious inscription was uncovered, apparently in old Tamil; and is the only inscription yet discovered in Anuradhapura which is not in Sinhalese or Nágara.

The next point of interest is the "Kuṭṭam pokuna", or twin bathing ponds (4¼ miles), the largest of which measures 132 ft. long by 51 ft. wide. The flights of steps on the N.W. and S. sides of the nearer "pokuna" are very effective and well preserved. Those in the farther pond are simpler in design but admirably executed. The moulding on the outside of the balustrade of each of the flights is well worth looking at, as is the construction of the front and back walls of the farther "pokuna", which are very well preserved. Notice, too, the very quaint drainage pipe supported on a lion, near the N.W. corner of this "pokuna". Part of this "pokuna" has been excellently restored by Mr. R. W. Ievers (Government Agent); and the accuracy and finish of the old stonework can now be appreciated. A jungle track, formerly the road to Mannar, leaves the northern end of the further "pokuna", and, after about three quarters of a mile, passes on the right the remains of an ancient Sinhalese bridge, formed entirely of large blocks of granite, which here crossed some natural or artificial watercourse. The remains are about 60 yards in length, and the stones have been wonderfully little displaced.

The main road passes no more ruins until it leads past the Abhayagiriya ("mountain of safety") dágoba (53¾ miles). When entire, this was the most stupendous dágoba in Ceylon. It was originally 180 cubits, or 405 feet high; its dome was hemispherical, and described with a radius of 180 ft. giving a circumference of 1,130 feet. Its summit was therefore 50 ft. higher than St. Paul's, and 50 feet lower than St. Peter's. At present it measures about 231 feet from the platform to the top of the sphere. The dágoba had fallen into such disrepair, that the engineers sent to examine it by the late Governor (Sir A. Gordon) reported its total collapse as probable and imminent. It was therefore partially restored by prison labour chiefly under the superintendence of Mr. Murray, P. W. D.; and the visitor can now easily ascend to the top of the platform, and thence, by an inner stairway to the interior of the pinnacle, and obtain an unrivalled view of the surrounding country The diameter at the base of the bell is about 325 feet, and at the outer, circle or basement 357 feet. The area of the platform on which it stands is about 8 acres, and the total area enclosed by the outer boundary wall about 11 acres. This vast building was erected by King Walagam Báhu in B.C. 89, to commemorate the recovery of his throne after the expulsion of the Malabar invaders. There is a fine entrance on the east side, but the chapel is quite hidden by the ruined brickwork ; and on the north side the chapel has almost disappeared ; but the western chapel presents some beautiful specimens of stone carving, a gigantic seven-headed cobra and two large male and female figures being well contrasted with the simple and effective flower patterns. The southern chapel is also in tolerable preservation ; here are two large stone cobras, of slightly different design, and various fragments of bold frescoes. The dágoba is quite encircled with the ruins of buildings large and small ; for a larger college of priests was attached to this than to any of the other sacred places in Anuradhapura.

A great deal of excavation has been done round this dágoba, since the first edition of this book was published, under the able superintendence of the Archæological Commissioner, Mr. H. C. P. Bell, c.s. The visitor is referred to his interesting reports to Government (procurable at the Colonial Secretary's Office, Colombo), and to the plans and drawings with which they are illustrated. Space forbids the insertion here of more than the following extract from the Second Report :—

"Within a quarter of a mile of the Abhayagiri, the sites of sacred buildings (the majority now only recognisable by their stone boundaries and pillar stumps) are clustered thick. Those bordering the roads have been, as might be expected, ruthlessly indented on for modern requirements. It may yet be possible, by a prompt survey, to ascertain with some degree of certainty the extent and position of many of these ruins, the habitation of one of the three chief Buddhistic establishments at Anuradhapura. But unless steps are taken without delay it will be hopeless to assay the task. A good deal—most indeed—of the land near the Abhayagiriya is now in private hands, and the owners have not been restrained by scruples of superstition or art from breaking up and carting away wholesale, boundary stones, pillars, steps, &c.—all, in short, that could be turned to profitable use. Under the circumstances, the wonder rather is that sufficient remains to allow of the *disjecta membra* being reduced to any order.

"It is with the greater satisfaction, therefore, that I am able to report two interesting discoveries in the midst of a general *bouleversement* which has resulted in semi-chaos.

" The first is the possible identification of the convent of the Abhayagiri Fraternity :

"(*a*) About 200 yards from the Native Resthouse, on the main road to Trincomalee and Kandy, a shapeless crowd of thick stone piers, ranging from 6 ft. to 6 in. above the ground, and running down to the roadside at an awkward angle, must frequently have attracted passing attention. These piers are of disintegrated gneiss, pinkish-yellow in colour, like sandstone, and roughly squared to an average width of 1 ft. 10 in. Many bear wedge marks close to the ground, with which the substantial abutments of the neighbouring Malwatu-Oya bridge may not be unconnected.*

"When the piers had been freed of undergrowth, and a careful line-by-line scrutiny made with measure-

* In justice to Public Works officers it should be stated that every effort has been made, since the express orders of Government a few years back, to put a stop to the reckless resort to ruins for building stone.

ments, an elaborate plan of a spacious building, precisely laid out, gradually evolved itself. I annex a ground plan drawn by me to scale.

" The building had a frontage of 100 ft. with a depth of 52 ft. 4 in., and at the back a bay 43 ft. 2 in. by 25 ft. 3 in. A verandah, 6 ft. wide, ran round the building inside, and cut the interior space into four rooms, (i.) the central hall, 35 ft. by 28 ft. with (ii.), (iii.), tv·o rooms on either side (25 ft. by 23 ft.), and (iv.) a third behind (28 ft. by 18 ft.). The outer wall was strengthened by sixty-four pillars, probably bricked up ; those of the inner rooms— except (iv.). which had fourteen—by twenty-two pillars. Rooms (i), (ii.), (iii.) had six additional pillars, and (iv.) two. These may have divided the rooms into twenty-eight cells by cross walls, or have been free-standing columns as shown in the plan. The roof of the cloistered verandah was further supported at intervals by central pillars, perhaps supporting double arches. The main entrances, 11 ft. wide, were almost certainly on the east and west, though no steps are traceable above ground. A passage (21 ft by 9 ft.) led west from the northern wing connecting it with (v.), a small room (15 ft. by 14 ft.), itself united at right angles to (vi.), a porch (15 ft. by 12 it.), by a shorter passage (14 ft. by 10 ft.). The regular entrance into (vi.) was on the north, and there may have been a corresponding doorway into (v.) from the south. The proxmity of the pillars and their bulk almost certainly prove that the building was storeyed—probably more than once ; and all above the ground floor was doubtless constructed of wood. At the eastern boundary wall of the premises, 122 ft. from the main building, a roomy *mandapa* facing the Abhayagiri, about 52 square, with wide steps in and out and 2-ft. square figured blocks, admitted into the convent close, immediately opposite the monastery.

" No other single ruin of the magnitude is known near the Abhayagiri. It may not perhaps be rash, therefore, to regard the building as the veritable residence of the famous 'Dhammaruchi brethren' who shared with the Theravadi and Jetawanáráma monks the servile deference and lavish benefactions of kings and ministers.

" If this surmise be correct, a clue is at once found enabling the identification of the so-called 'elephant stables' near the Jetawanáráma, and the pillared building near the Miriswetiya to be similarly fixed.

" (b) To the west is a fair-sized *pokuna*, once stone-faced, but with nothing of its original adornment left, except two pairs of balustrades lying at the bottom upturned, and some casual pieces of the stone side walls and coping. Probably much of the stone work lies buried.

" (c) About fifty yards north-west of the *pokuna*, and abutting on the Outer Circular, were found an octagonal shaft and *puhul* capital (a type not hitherto noticed at Anuradhapura) and some narrow moulded slabs deeply morticed. These gave hope of further discovery. When the raised site, six or eight feet above ground level, and some 140 ft. in length by 110 ft. broad, had been cleared of scrub, search was rewarded by a valuable Archæological 'find'—a post with three rails attached, in two pieces—a genuine fragment of a structural 'Buddhist railing.' Fortunately the peculiar shape of the semiconvex rails had saved them from the fate of the shapely pillars of which but stumps remain in position. The tenons at both ends of the standard explained at once the purpose of the morticed slabs. Here were the rail, post, and plinth; only the coping seemed wanting. After continued search a portion of this was found, showing a few inches above ground, and close to it two slabs of a rounded basement, 10 in. in depth, as orgininally built at right angles to each other. This fixed the south-east corner and determined the plan of the railing which followed the lines of the oblong site. Trial excavations brought up more pieces of rails and coping, and two additional members—a stepped subplinth and a low socle below the quarter-round base. There is, therefore, every reason to hope that by running a trench along the foot of the mound, more of this fine railing will be unearthed, and that it may yet be possible to restore it in part to nearly its pristine form.

"The railing consisted of square 8 in. standards,—the angle posts probably 10 in. by 8 in.,—3 ft. 10 in. in height, kept upright by tenons (3 in. by 2 in.) at top and bottom, which fitted mortices in the upper plinth and coping. Three lenticular rails, $13\frac{1}{2}$ in. deep, project from the posts 9 in. to 12 in. The centre rail is separated $1\frac{1}{4}$ in. from the upper and lower rails, and these 2 in. from coping and plinth respectively. A thin tie ($1\frac{1}{2}$ in. by $\frac{1}{2}$ in.), strengthens the rails near their lateral extremities. The widest interspaces of the mortice holes on the plinth slabs are but 17 in., which would bring the posts within a foot of one another; some would seem to have been still closer together. The coping, rounded at top, is 8 in. deep, the upper plinth 13 in., and both are delicately moulded. The lower plinth, three-stepped ($2, 2\frac{1}{4}, 2\frac{3}{4}$ in.), is 7 in. in depth, the basement 8 in., and the socle 9 in.—all cut on their upper surface with a half-inch set to prevent the members above sagging outwards. The entire railing rested on a stone foundation, and from ground to coping was 7 ft. 6 in. in height.

" Comparing it with the best known Indian examples, it follows that at Buddha Gayá in being rectangular, therein differing from the Bharhut, Sanchi, and Amaravati rails. In unsculptured barrenness it resembles the railing round the Great Tope of Sanchi, but carries simplicity even further by square, in lieu of octagonal, posts".*

The outer circular road next passes the native rest-house, 6 miles, and so runs into the Mihintalé road. But instead of following this part of it, the visitor is recommended to leave the Abhayagiriya by the western side, and to make straight for the Ruwaṇveli, through a park-like stretch of undulating land, crossing the bed of an old irrigation channel, called the Halpan-ela, and passing on his right the so-called Sélachaittiya, or Kuja Tisa Dágoba, a small, but very sacred, structure, with some splendid remains of stone carving and stairways. The proper name of this little dágoba is probably " Lajjikavihára, " and it appears to have been erected by King Lajji-tissa,

---

* Mr. Burrows states (Report, Sessional Paper No. X. 1886, pp. 8, 12) that he came on a " Buddhist railing " when working at the *Nissanka Latá Mandapaya*, " perhaps the most interesting building in Polonnaruwa. " " Unfortunately it has been wilfully and extensively broken, but most of the stone posts are still standing, while on the western side two posts are left with their rails still in position, which enable us to form an excellent idea of the whole arrangement." From the measurements annexed to his Report the rail is shown to differ considerably from that just found at Anuradhapura, being rather of "post and rail" type in stone. The posts are higher (5 ft. 5 in.), though of much the same width (8 in. by 8¾ in.). But the rails are both longer (3 ft. 2¼ in.), more shallow (7½ in.), and half an inch thicker (6 in.), and the interspace runs from 6 in to 10¾ in.

a nephew of King Duṭugẹmunu, about B.C. 119, to mark
a place where Buddha is said to have rested; but for
some reason or other, it has long been known as the
Sélachaiṭṭiya (stone temple), a name which properly
belongs to a dágoba at the Mihintalé mountain. In
general design and outline, it is curiously similar to,
though more ornate than, the newly-discovered Wijayá-
ráma Dágoba.

Three roads in connection with the outer circular
road remain to be described. The first of these leaves the
outer circular directly after the third mile-stone, and
passes between a pair of small twin "pokunas" known as
the "Tammettan pokuna" ("Tammettan" being a pair
of kettledrums or small round tomtoms in common use
among Sinhalese musicians). Soon after leaving the
elephants' "pokuna" on the left, the visitor will see on his
right a fine stone gateway, on the fringe of the jungle;
and about fifteen yards beyond this, on the same side, a
little path leads to what is known as the "gal-gé," or
stone-house. Passing through a collection of stone
pillars, a fine, ruined stairway,* the path leads at once to
a long rounded hummock of natural rock, which must
have been extensively quarried in former times, as it is
covered with the marks of the wedges used to break off
the slabs of stone. Underneath the east side of the rock
three small chambers have been excavated and partially
walled in with brick: these were probably the cells of
ascetics. Nearly opposite is a plain "patula" stone, a
platform with twenty-four pillars, and a well-preserved

* Opposite to this stairway, there is a half-finished moonstone; the semi-circular lines and a few devices only being com
pleted and others merely sketched. The workmen were possibly
disturbed at their work by the invaders, and never returned to it.

stairway. On the right of the road leading from the "gal-
gé" to the Lankárama Dágoba, a fine building has been
discovered. Its base is square, with a broad "gangway"
of smooth granite slabs running along its four sides. The
moulding and finish of the outer walls are admirable; and
the doorway is unique, being formed of two upright slabs
of granite, about 8 feet high by $3\frac{1}{2}$ feet wide and 5 inches
thick, with a false pillar represented on each. There are
four annexes at the four corners, with decorated stairways
and "door guardians;" a vast "pokuna" to the south, and
a large dágoba, (or natural hill transformed into a dágoba)
on the west. The "gal-gé" rock is close to on the north.
The Mahawaṇso (Chap. 21.) states that King Suratissa,
who reigned B.C. 247-237, built a Vihare close to the
Tangùttaro hill (the "gal-gé"), which may probably be
identified with this one. It is particularly stated that
"this ruler of the land caused this and other viharas
"to be built in great perfection, without causing any
"oppression." The jungle to the south and east of the
"gal-gé" is full of ruins and enclosures, possibly marking the site of the buildings which connected the Maha
Vihare, or sacred town, with the secular part of the city.

The visitor will find more recent information as to
the "gal-gé" and its surroundings in Mr. Bell's Third
Archæological Report.

Returning again to the road, the visitor will soon
arrive at a small dágoba called the Lankáráma, said by
tradition to have been erected by Prakrama Báhu, as
late as the twelfth century A.D. The northern side
of this dágoba has fallen away, and exposes to view
the manner in which some at least of these dágobas
were built. There are the remains of a low altar at

each of the cardinal points; and a treble row of very delicate and classic pillars, with 20, 28 and 40 pillars in each row respectively. They resemble the pillars at the Thupáráma, but are all monolithic. Notice the exquisite finish of the lion and goose designs on the capitals. There is a fine stone waterpipe, cut in the shape of a mythical beast, near the S.-E. side of the dágoba, and several mutilated statues of Buddha at the S.-E. corner of the enclosure. Pillars marking the dwellings of the priests are to be seen at the N.-W. corner, and on the southern side of the road. Leaving the Lankáráma, the visitor will emerge on the road which runs northwards to the Jétawanáráma, and southward to the Inner circular and Thúpáráma.

Another expedition to be made from the outer circular is by a path which runs due north through the jungle from the northern side of the Jétawanáráma to some very interesting ruins which have only recently been discovered, distant about 2 miles. The path leads first to a small dágoba, not unlike, in general design, the so-called Sélachaittiya in Anuradhapura, *i.e.*, the dágoba itself rises from the centre of a square platform about 50 feet by 50, with a boundary wall of plain slabs of stone, about 2½ feet high, with four stairways or approaches; the carving on which is markedly plain compared with analogous specimens in Anuradhapura. A deep hole has been dug into the centre of the dágoba itself, probably by villagers in search of treasure. It must originally have stood some 20 feet high, with a diameter at the base of about 30 feet. To the north and west of this dágoba there are a great many ruins, the most remarkable of which is a large oblong platform, about 80 feet by 50. There are no signs of pillars upon it, but on the huge slabs which form the boundary wall are some beautiful specimens of stone-carving of a simple and uniform design—a single upright male figure under a heavy canopy in very high relief. Both the general plan of this building, and the massive designs on the entablature are obviously different from any of the ruins in Anuradhapura, nor is there any trace of a connexion between the two places ; but, while these differences are obvious, the identification of the site is at present little more than a guess. About half a mile to the North of this place is a huge grass mound which covers another dágoba known as the Kiribat Vehera.

In 1891, the Archæological Commissioner began a fresh investigation of this site ; and the following extract from his Fourth Report will be read with interest :—

" The jungle had grown up everywhere since 1884, and necessitated fresh cutting. This has now been done, and the clearing extended well back on all sides, so as to open out the entire monastery including the majority of off-buildings standing outside the boundary wall of the inner enclosure. The area cleared embraces some 300 yards square.

" As the jungle was cut back, the perfect symmetrical arrangement of this fine monastery gradually developed itself.

" In general plan it somewhat resembles the monas-tery at Toluwila. A similar raised quadrangle, with en-trances at the four cardinal points: within, a dágoba located east, one or two vihares and ' annexes ' dotted round outside. But beyond these broad features the re-semblance well-nigh ends. In lieu of the elevated *pilimagé* (image-house) and *wata-dá-gé* of Toluwila situated respectively S.-E. & N.-W., within the walled enclosure, here are two buildings both rectangular and on level ground with tall, slender, squared pillars. The number and location of the exterior annexes and of the pansala also differs. No far reaching street, as at Toluwila, conducts to the latter. The Maha Thera of ' Vijayáráma ' Pirivena resided within easy distance of the sacred precincts and his daily ministrations.

" Pending a survey of the ' Vijayáráma ' Monastery by the officers of the Survey Department, I have prepared a ground plan, drawn to scale, which will be useful in explaining the following description* :—

" Approaching from the south along a street marked on one side by a line of stones, which commences at the site of some building (possibly an ambalam), 120 yards distant from the monastery precincts (*a*), the *mura-gé*, or entrance lodge, is reached. This is a building on twelve stout pillars roughly hewn, and from it a plain boundary of large single stones, not continuous, runs east and west.

" Passing through the lodge (*a*) still north along the street for about 20 yards, on the right are some low steps leading off by a street to a large building (*b*) of 48 pillars (46 by 38 by 3).† The building was entered on the west front by three sets of steps which admitted into a corridor, perhaps open, 5 ft. 6 in. in width, encircling the walled building proper (33 ft 6 in. by 25 ft.

---

* " Not reproduced. The delay in the issue of this Report enables me to give the survey plan of the Monastery before excavation commenced. In the Report for the Second Quarter of 1891, will appear a detailed plan of the site as exhumed."

† " Surface measurement, as in all cases prior to excavation."

9 in.), which was supported on 24 columns, giving 8 ft.
6 in. passage down the centre west and east. The pillars
are 7 ft. in height and squared to 8 in., with the exception
of the eight at the angles of the corridor and inner building, which are 10 ft. by 10 in. It may be assumed that
this was the main *pansala*.

"Between this *pansala* and the monastery walls are
two rows of short piers (*c*), of some minor building.

"Directly west of (*b*), and across the Main street, is
another building (*d*), similar as regards the number of
pillars (at present only 5 ft. high), 50 ft. in length by 34
ft. broad. If there were steps, they are below ground,
but the entrance was almost certainly on the east or north
side. Between (*d*) and the uttermost of the stone walls—
three on the south side—which enclose the monastery
quadrangle is a small stone-faced *pokuṇa*, or may be a
well, 17 ft. square ; and lying between the first and second
boundary lines (counting outwards) seem to have been
several small outhouses (privies, &c.), skirting the south-
east corner, and shut off from view by separate stone
walls.

"A width of 68 ft. separates the second stone boundary from the first or nearest stone wall to the monastery
enclosure. Within this piazza were built twelve 'annexes,' all exactly alike in every respect (about 17
ft. square, surface measurement), balancing one another
on the four sides with a regularity and fitness which
is admirable. On either side of the approach to each
of the four flights of steps (north, south, east, and
west) leading up to the monastery are placed two, facing
inward, and hanging off its angles to complete the dozen,

four more, two fronting east, two west. Of two (*s.v.*), hardly a vestige remains, whilst not a single one retains all its pillars intact.*

" Behind that (*q*) at the north-west corner of the monastery, fifty yards away, are 24 stone piers, in two rows, with a double line of rough stone in front.

" Besides the small pond, two other larger *pokunu* served the monastery—one immediately behind, ' annexe ' (*u*) on the east, the other and biggest of the three fifty yards north.

" The third line of boundary on the south is of single rough stones, but the second and first nearing the monastery are formed of worked slabs, ovolo-shaped or quarter round, on the inner face.

" The third line is united with the second at right angles on either side of the south steps, leaving a fine approach nearly 40 ft. wide.

" This passage leads direct to the steps by which access is gained to the monastery quadrangle, a temenos, 95 yards north and south, 88 yards east and west, raised throughout 6 or 8 ft. above the level of the ground around. It was originally encircled by a wall of brick pierced, after the Toluwila plan, by two stone *pili*, or spouts, on each face. At no point is this brick wall standing now. The *débris* falling outwards has transformed the once

* " 'Annexe' *m*, has 3 stumps of pillars ; *n*, 3 complete standing pillars, and 5 stumps ; *o*, 12 stumps ; *p*, 12 stumps ; *q*, 1 complete pillar, and 10 stumps ; *r*, 12 stumps ; *s*, none ; *t*, 1 complete pillar and 11 stumps ; *u*, 1 fallen pillar complete. and 10 stumps ; *v*, none ; *w*, 3 complete pillars standing, 1 complete pillar fallen, and 7 stumps ; *x*, 12 stumps."

level *piṭa' vidiya,* 17 ft. in width, which encircled the sacred enclosure between this raised inner wall and the first boundary line of stone, into a gentle slope, where the foot stumbles at every step over the outcrop of brickwork.

"At the head of the three flights of steps into the monastery on the south, east, and west sides, and also on the north though without a stairway, projecting from the line of the brick enclosing wall are porticos (*d, e, f, g,*) of twelve stone pillars 17 ft. square. Each stairway consists of ten steps without balustrades, but flanked (at the south and west flight at least,) by large guard-stones figured with the same obese dwarf janitors made familar by the well-known pair at the southern *maṇḍapa* of the Jéta-wanáráma dágoba.

"Entering within the limits of the originally walled enclosure by the south porch, to the right, abutting against the east boundary a few feet south of the eastern portico, is a striking mound on which large trees have grown (*h*). This is banked by a quadrilateral revetment of great stone slabs boldly moulded 47 ft. 6 in. square. The moulding follows one of the ordinary graceful Anuradhapura types. A rectangular sockle, ovolo plinth, plain block dispensing with a torus, completed by ogee and stepped coping.

"This square platform formed the stylobate of the *dágoba,* the tholobate of which must lie beneath the coating of earth and tree roots of the present mound. A solid low single-course parapet, 10 in. in height, with quarter-round inner face similar to the slabs of the first boundary line of stone one finishes the elevation of the platform.

"Perrons of 10 steps stand out from the plane of the revetment on all four sides. The steps are finished at their sides by unornamented balustrades running down into volutes and a pair of " vase-pattern " terminals. The design of the vase is of a different type than that (*e.g.*, the steps near the Court-house) noticeable usually in Anuradhapura ruins. Here diagonal lines are made to cross the vases. The long exposure to the elements has weathered the surface carving greatly.

"From the level of the top step the mound rises irregularly. Down its centre a wide pit has been sunk at some former period, when no doubt the dágoba was sacked. From the examination of the sides of the shaft as left by the wreckers it is to be gathered that the dágoba was not built throughout of bricks laid in courses, though there are signs of brickwork having covered a width of about two yards square at the centre, with a filling or gravel and rubble extending to the outer shell.

"In the south-west corner of the quadrangle stood a building (*i*), on 16 pillars with 8 extra pillars, (on each face two), 34 ft. 9 in. by 33 ft. entered perhaps on all four sides, though there are no steps.

"North of the west entrance, but more centrally placed than (*i*), is another building (*j*), somewhat smaller in itself (26 ft. 3 in. by 26 ft.), but from the presence of six additional pillar stumps on its south side, evidently augmented by a pronaos (18 ft. 2 in. by 11 ft.) with a flight of steps projecting 7 ft. outside. The pillars of the building run from 9 in. to 6½ in. in girth, and in proportion are exceptionally tall, 10 ft. 5 in. Until they can be excavated, it would be rash to surmise what special purpose these two buildings served, though they are not improbably image houses.

" A third building (*k*), however, on 24 shaped columns, 7 ft. in height by 9 in. square, situated north-west of the east steps, 'was without doubt a *vihâre*. It resembles in every particular *vihâre* already described in previous reports. The building is in length 34 ft. by 26 ft. and has evidently a landing and flight of steps buried on the south side, for a portion of one guard-stone shows above ground.

" The three buildings (*i, j, k,*) and the dágoba (*h*) are apparently the only structures actually within the en-closure. But connected with it at the north porch by raised ground (possibly a regular passage) is a great oblong hypethral ' hall ' on the same level, 68 ft. 6 in. in depth by 52 ft. broad. This is the ' monastery,' or ' palace,' so called by Mr. Burrows. Excavation may help to determine its object. This open building must have been walled in by massive slabs capped by a heavy moulded coping. At present the stonework, nearly all which has fallen inwards, is lying half buried, and much of it will have to be grubbed out of the roots of large trees that have sprung up inside the building and round its walls.

"The basement is more than half underground, but is certainly moulded throughout. From this rose two slab courses with their coping. Two or three slabs on the south front seem to have been set up by Mr. Burrows : the rest thrown backward, peep out from the soil here .and there

" The building was drained by gurgoyle spouts passing out through the wall below slab course, the bottom of which ran level with the floor within the building.

" From the dimensions of such slabs, as it is possible at present to measure, it may be asserted that the building, if walled in completely on all four sides, would have had eight slabs on the front and back faces, and eleven on each of its sides.

"The plan of the building itself and the ornamentation of its walls is in a style widely divergent from that of the ruined vihàras around the Anuradhapura dágobas. In their absence of elaboration, they partake rather of the simplicity noticeable at Isurumuniya. The general design of the ornament resembles somewhat a series of " cameos " in granite, with vertical raised bands of flowered carving at intervals, carried round the exterior face of the walls. Above the " cameos " of standing figures carved in sunk relief—no part rising above the plane of the surrounding surface—are *makara toran* in *messo relievo*, differing in detail."

The visitor should next proceed about half-a-mile down the Kurunegala road to a very interesting and ancient temple called Isurumuniya, which was constructed by King Dewenipiatissa about 300 B.C. The temple is carved out of, and circles round, an abrupt formation of natural rock; and its shrine is approached by two terraces, the steps and janitors being in excellent preservation. The outer wall of the upper terrace is ornamented with a most remarkable series of seventeen mural frescoes in low relief, the subjects being grotesque to the last degree. Notice particularly the large tablet on the south wall, consisting of a group of three women, a man and an attendant; and near it the group of three grotesque men seated; and on the north wall the group of three figures, one playing a musical instrument. On the southern face of the lower terrace there is a sculpture precisely similar to these, but on a larger scale; the stone measuring 2 ft. 3 in. by 3 ft. 1 in. Notice also the bold gurgoyle forming a waterspout at the base of the south wall, and the stone lion beaneath, which evidently supported a drainage pipe. Close to the entrance to the shrine, on the right hand side, is a large sitting figure in high relief, holding a horse, and carved out of the face of the rock; and underneath it, just above the small "pokuna," are the heads of four elephants in low relief; the outline of the right hand one being very quaintly designed. The stone doorway is a fine specimen of carving, and deserves minute inspection. Notice, too, the beautiful proportion of the pillars which support the porch in front of it. The shrine itself has lately been painted in the gaudiest style of native art. The sedent figure in the centre (4 ft. 2 in. high), together with its pedestal and surrounding ornamentation, is cut from the solid rock. The two figures on either side, in the attitude of exhoration, are of wood, but of ancient workmanship. Close to the southern base of the lower terrace is the "pansala," or priests' dwelling-house; and between it and the rock itself is a curious little "gal-gé" or rock-cut room. At the northern end of the rock is a small bó-tree planted in a crevice, with a low altar near it for flower offerings; and on the eastern side is a flight of steps leading to the summit, where there is a "sripatula," or sacred foot-mark of Buddha, recently cut in imitation of the celebrated one on Adam's Peak. It is needless to dwell with regret upon the

debased attempts at modern architecture which disfigure
the summit of this unique and magnificent rock temple.
The grotesque character of the Isurumuniya frescoes
forming so distinct a contrast to the usual ornamentation
around a shrine sacred to Buddha, demands a fuller explanation than can be found in the scanty records of the
Mahawaṇso.

About a quarter of a mile further down the Kuruṇe-
gala road, a little jungle path to the left leads to another
huge boulder of rock, and underneath its eastern shoulder
are some remains of rude rock dwellings known tradition-
ally as the Nunnery, with the ruins of some connected
buildings in close proximity. It is at least clear from
the Mahawaṇso that King Duṭugẹmunu constructed
some dwellings for female recluses in this immediate
neighbourhood.* The visitor can vary his return journey
by going back to Isurumuniya, ascending the high bank
on the western side of the rock, and walking along the
bund of Tisávewa into Anuradhapura.

Space forbids more than a bare allusion to the
interesting monastic ruins of Puliyankulama, which lie at
the apex of the triangle formed by the Trincomalee road,
the Jaftna road, and the deviation, about two miles and
a half from the town : and of Toluvila, which lie about
half a mile N. of the Ayton Road, and about two miles
S.-E. of the town. The visitor, who has time to spend
on these ruins, is referred to Mr. Bell's Sixth and First
progress reports.

* Mahawaṇso, xx., 20.

CHAPTER IV.

MIHINTALE.

EIGHT miles to the East of Anuradhapura, the solitary mountain of Mihintalé rises abruptly from the jungle-covered plain. The road to it, passing between the Brazen Palace and the resthouse, skirts a part of the bund of Nuwara-vẹwa (the "city tank") bet˜ ween the second and third mile-posts. This noble tank is said to be the Jayavẹwa, mentioned in the Maha-waṇso as having been constructed by King Pandukhábaya about 400 B.C. It has been recently restored. At Mihintalé there is a small resthouse, where ordinary supplies can be got if ordered beforehand. The mountain itself was possibly the scene of an ancient hill-worship anterior to the introduction of Buddhism. Its sanctity in the eyes of Buddhists is due to the fact that on its summit alighted the great missionary prince, Mahindo,* when arriving from India to preach the

* See part I.

tenets of the new faith, B.C. 307. Soon after his arrival, King Dewenipiatissa, who was out hunting on the mountain, was miraculously allured to approach the place where Mahindo sat ; and after hearing a discourse from him, was promptly converted to Buddhism, together with forty thousand of his followers. Mahindo died on the mountain, B.C. 267.

A guide should be procured from the resthouse to the foot of the ascent, nearly a mile distant. A flight of steps formed of huge slabs of granite, and said to be 1,840 in number, leads from the base to the summit. These steps are arranged in four flights. At the top of the first flight a narrower stairway to the right conducts to the remains of some cave dwellings. Half way up the third flight, a narrow path to the left leads to the remains of a curious stone aqueduct supported on stone pillars; beyond which is an enormous stone trough, in good preservation, probably used to hold food for priests. A little farther up the mountain, a small flight of steps to the left leads to the ruins of an important shrine. Two slabs measuring 7 ft. high by 4 wide and 2 thick, clear of the frames, stand upright at the entrance and are covered with inscriptions of the late 10th century. At the top of the third fight of steps are the remains of the *Bhójana Sáláwa* or refectory of the priests. Near the middle of the last flight of steps a narrow path to the right leads to the "Nága Pokuna", or snake-bathing-place. This is formed out of the solid rock and measures about 130 ft. in length. At the back, a five-headed cobra has been carved out of the rock in high relief, and is represented as rising from the water. It measures nearly 7 ft. high, and 6 ft. across the head, and is a striking piece of realistic stone carving. Passing by the "Nága Pokuna", the path leads on to the Etwehera, the dágoba which crowns the summit of the highest peak of Mihintalé. Returning from the " Nága Pokuna" to the main stairway, the visitor will notice, nearly at the top of the fourth flight of steps, a curious inscription, in very large letters, cut on the rock to the right of the path. The king whose name occurs in this fine inscription is called "Gámini Abhaya", who may be either Gaja Báhu I., A.D. 113, or Méghawarna, A D. 254 : Dr. Müller thinks the latter date the more probable. The path then ascends to the " Mura Maduwa " or guard-house, which leads on to the picturesque platform that surrounds the Ambustála dágoba. This dágoba marks the scene of the first inter-view between Mabindo and his royal convert Deweni-piatissa, and is said to contain the ashes of the great missionary. It is built of stone instead of brick; the terrace round it being encircled with octagonal pillars, the capitals of which are ornamented with carvings of the sacred goose. Some fine stone capitals lie on the ground close by, on which alternate figures of grotesque men and geese are carved. To the south of the Ambustála is a broken stone statue, said to be of King Deweni-piatissa, and undoubtedly of great antiquity. The coco-nut trees close to it afford a pleasant drink after the toil-some ascent. Nearly opposite the statue, notice the curious oblong cuttings in the rock, supposed to be the beginnings of cave dwellings, never completed. One more flight of steps leads to the gallery surrounding the Mahaséya dágoba, which was built over a single hair which grew between Buddha's eyebrows. This dágoba was partially restored during the governorship of Sir Arthur Gordon to prevent its utter collapse. The view from the gallery—or, for the adventurous climber, from the summit—of this dàgoba is extremely striking; to the west, the three great dágobas of Anuradhapura emerge from the sea of foliage, and the glittering waters of Tissavęwa and Nuwaravęwa are a relief to the unending green; to the south the plain is broken by the hill of " Katiwarakande," and the rugged outline of Ritigala. Descending again to the Ambustála, the visitor should quit the platform by a little path exactly opposite to the " Mura Maduwa " and keeping almost due east for about quarter of a mile, he will come to a curious arch hollowed out of a narrow granite clift and terminated by a flat slab, which is known as " Mahindo's bed." Though its properties as a couch are uninviting, the situation is most romantic. To the left is a deep ravine filled with great boulders of granite half covered by creepers; to the right the view stretches to the verge of the horizon over an unbroken expanse of jungle foliage. Just below are some curious rock chambers, once the dwellings of hermits, and now the trysting-place for multitudes of bats.

When the visitor descends the mountain again, and emerges from the jungle path on to the Tirappane road, he should turn to the left, and a walk of a few hundred yards will bring him to another collection of ruins, containing two small dágobas, (the nearer one being known as the Sélachaittiya), a " pokuna" with a stone aqueduct, and numerous walls and enclosures. Some beautiful specimens of maiden-hair and silver fern are to be found growing in the crumbling brickwork.

Continuing about a quarter of a mile farther down the same road, a plank crosses the ditch to the lefthand side, and a narrow path leads to the Kaludiya (" black water") pokuna. Though mostly artificial, this " pokuna" has all the beauties of a natural lake. The water is of a considerable depth, the trees fringe its edge, and there are many curious stone ruins and indistinct remains beside its banks.

CHAPTER V.

KALAVEWA.

WITH a day to spare, the visitor is strongly recommended to pay a visit to Kalá-Balaḷuvẹwa, on his way to or from Anuradhapura. This gigantic tank is the reservoir which ultimately supplies Anuradhapura with water, being connected with that place by a winding canal called the Yóda-ela or giant's canal, 54 miles in length, which on its way feeds a widely-extended system of village tanks. The tank itself (or rather tanks, for though originally distinct, Kaláveẉa and Balaḷuvẹwa are now connected by a breach) is fed from the projecting spurs of the northern end of the hill district ; the Dambul Oya and the Mirisgoni Oya being the two largest feeders. The double tank has a total area of 4,425 acres, or about 7 square miles, with a contour of 30 miles. Natural high ground runs round the greater part of it, but an enormous bund or artificial bank runs along the western side, measuring six miles in length, with a breadth of 20 feet at the top, and an average height of 60 feet. It is formed of large blocks of stone and earthwork, and provided with a fine spill-wall, 260 feet long, 200 wide, and about 40 feet high. Close to the spill-wall is a collection of very curious and unique pillars ; each pillar is in two sections, which are connected by a double mortice and tenon joint : while the joints are further strengthened by stone collars, one or two of which are still nearly in position. When the tank was full, these pillars must have been very deeply immersed, though they are over 17 feet high ; and there is no trace of any connexion with the higher part of the bund. It has been conjectured that they supported a seat from which the King looked over the tank ; but perhaps some light may by thrown upon the purpose they served by the following passage from the Mahawaṇso, which refers to the tank at Anuradhapura, now known as Basawakulam :—" Moreover King Duṭugẹmunu placed pillars in the water of Abhavẹwa and caused that celebrated preaching hall to be built upon them : and who shall describe the halls which he caused to be built in the air ? "*

Just beyond the spill-wall is the great breach, 1,000 feet broad, which destroyed the utility of the tank at some unknown period. Whether this was caused by a heavy flood, or by the malevolence of the Tamil invader, or of a neighbouring Rája, it is impossible to decide. The first supposition is the more probable, as the part of the bund which has been breached rested on a foundation of natural rock, and was probably insecurely fixed into it. The tank was constructed by Rája Dhátu Séna A.D. 460. The sluice and the well, or " bisokotua," are still in wonderful preservation, the latter being 12 feet square and 25 feet

* Sinhalese translation, ch. xxvi., par. 19-21.

deep, faced with enormous plain slabs running its whole length.   These are bounded in a most peculiar manner, and backed with brickwork.   The channel running from it under the bund conducts the water into the "Yoda-ẹla" canal, and so to Anuradhapura.

To reach Kalávẹwa, the visitor should stop at Kekiráwa, the first stage (14 miles) out of Dambulla, where the resthouse is excellent, and supplies can be got if ordered by letter two days beforehand.   Sleeping there the night, a guide should be procured, and an early start made next morning, either on foot or horseback, along a pleasant and easy village path, about 5 miles to the bund, and 7 to the spill-wall of the tank, or by the new high road to Kalávẹwa, which is about 1½ mile longer.   There is no resthouse accommodation here, but failing an introduction to the Public Works Officer in charge, a shed can easily be procured to breakfast, and even to sleep, in, provisions and bed being carried by coolies.   The coach stops at Kekiráwa, both going at 9 p.m., and returning at 4-30 a.m.

Kalávẹwa has other interests : engineering, archæological and picturesque.   Firstly, Government has undertaken the restoration of this tank and its canal.   A huge masonary wall has been thrown across the breach of the tank, and an additional piece of bund thrown out to meet it.   The bund of the Yoda-ẹla canal has been repaired, partly by Tamil labour, partly by Sinhalese villagers selected from the various "korales" or shires which will benefit by its water.   The restoration cost altogether over half a million of rupees, and took about three years. It is perhaps the grandest experiment in irrigation ever undertaken in modern Ceylon.   Its completion means the resuscitation of the most important part of the North-Central Province, the second largest province in the island. The tank will hold about 20 feet of water, which not only water the great ranges of fields which stretch away from the bund, but are carried down the winding " Yoda-ẹla " canal for 54 miles, supplying innumerable village tanks on its way ; and ultimately fill the " Tisávẹwa " tank at Anuradhapura so completely as to enable the town lands to defy the dreaded years of drought. The restoration of this tank was due to the enlightened irrigation policy of Sir Arthur Gordon (Lord Stanmore), by whom it was opened in 1888 with an imposing ceremonial.

Secondly, there are two very interesting ruins within reach. The first of these is the so-called Vijitapura, which lies close to the northern end of the bund, and which can be seen on the way from Kekiráwa to the spill wall, if the guide is instructed accordingly. If the remains be those of the first Vijitapura, the settlement dates from 500 B.C , and is called after a brother-in-law of King Panduwasa, who was a nephew of the original invader Wijaya. It was a fortress and a city when Anuradhapura was still a village, and, according to the Mahawaṇso, was surrounded by a triple battlement, and entered by a gate of iron.

A flight of twelve stone steps, each bearing the remains of an inscription apparently in the Nágara charater, but almost defaced by time and the feet of pilgrims, leads up to a cleared space, from the centre of which rises a well-preserved dágoba, from 40 to 50 feet high, with a diameter of about 90 feet. A stone enclosure runs all round it, and there is a small inner enclosure on the north

side, containing "a bana-gé," or preaching hall, the
bottom step of which has been worn down quite two
inches by pious knees and feet. To the north of this
enclosure are the foundation pillars of a "piriwena," or
monastery for priests, with two entrances in a line and
door-guardians carved on the entrance stones. Round
the dágoba there are four altars, and underneath is said
to be hidden the jawbone of Buddha. There are niches
for lamps all round the top of the dágoba balustrade.
The surrounding jungle is full of pillars and remains of
buildings.

The second place of interest is the Aūkana Vihare.
This is situated 2½ miles to the N.-W. of the spill-wall.
The path leads through thick jungle, and across the bed
of the Kala Oya—the stream which carries off the water
from the breach in the bund of Kaláv̥ewa—to a collection
of square abrupt rocks which stand out boldly on the top
of a low hill. From one of these rocks, an enormous
upright figure of Buddha has been carved. It measures 33
ft. 3 in. from its pedestal, and is beautifully executed
and preserved. Every detail of the robe and limbs is
fresh and accurate, and the expression of the face and
pose of the figure combine an idea of majesty and repose.
The statue is slightly joined to the rock behind it by a
narrow strip at the back. It faces due east, and when
the intervening jungle was padi-land irrigated from Kalá-
v̥ewa, it must have been plainly visible from the bund,
at which it gazes. Near the right foot (which is 6 feet
long) lies a square slab with a cobra carved on it in high
relief. There are several small dágobas and enclosures
facing the statue.

When the workmen were repairing the top of the Kalávęwa bund, just above the Yodi-ęla sluice, they came across a rusty iron broad-sword, with a two-edged blade, 3 feet in length, and a fairly perfect but very narrow hilt, buried about two feet deep. Close to it were the still more rusty remains of a dagger blade and some grotesque heads made of clay. The sword is exactly similar in shape to those carried by the attendants of King Duṭu-gemunu in the picture of his conflict with Elála in the big temple at Dambulla.

CHAPTER VI

MINNERI AND POLONARUWA.

THE journey to Polonaruwa is a more serious undertaking than the expeditions already described, and visitors contemplating it are strongly advised to write to the Government Agent at Anuradhapura beforehand and enquire as to the state of the roads and ask for the assistance of the headmen, on whose good will the possibility of obtaining supplies depends. It is not a trip to be undertaken without full preparation and enquiry, and is a trying one for ladies.

The new cart road branches off from Habarane rest-house (15 miles from Dambulla down the Trincomalee cart road), and is now open as far as Topare or Topávęwa, which is equivalent to Polonaruwa. It is practicable for wheeled traffic most of the year. It crosses the two spills of Minneriya tank (15 miles from Habarane), and from the second spill you get a good view of Sígiriya rock. The road to the Tank bungalow (unfurnished) at Minneriya tank turns off to the right close to the 15th mile-post. It is nearly a mile to the bungalow; and the détour is well worth making.

This huge tank is said to have been made or repaired by King Mahá Séna* towards the end of the third century A.D. ; it is about 20 miles in circumference, with an artificial bund of 5 miles long and 60 feet high. The sluices are on a level with the deepest parts of the tank, and are never closed. It was formerly a noted place for game of all descriptions ; but cheap guns and gunpowder have greatly thinned their numbers. However, there is generally a herd of elephants in the vicinity ; and deer, snipe and teal can be got if there is time to go after them. The view of the lake at sunset, with its hanging woods and distant hills, is strikingly beautiful ; and has been compared by Sir E. Tennent to the glories of Killarney.

In the village itself is situated the temple of King Mahá Sena*: it is a most humble mud hut, containing only one relic worth looking at, a curious iron sword with a square hilt, and ornamented with small brass chains: but it is interesting from the extraordinary reverence with which it is regarded, on account of the dreaded memory of the deified King Even at the present day a rude kind of justice is administered at this shrine. A man accused of a crime will probably demand the right to clear himself by swearing before the image of Maha Sen. He and his accuser then resort to the temple, and, after a cursory examination, the Kapurála or officiating priest recommends one party, or both, to go through with the ordeal. Before taking the oath, the night must be passed in an open shed near the temple ; and as this is exposed to the numerous wild beasts and to the malarial exhalations of the neighbourhood, the god has not un-

* See Part I., page 9.

frequently been known to show his discrimination by incapacitating the guilty party from taking the morning oath. The visitor should get a guide from the village to show him the rude shrine on the top of the bund, where there are some antique and curious images of Maha Sen, his wife, and the god or genius of the tank. This is about a quarter of a mile from the Gansabawa by the short cut; and a little way below, and to the south of it, there is a circular stone enclosure containing an interesting collection of ancient pottery—propitiatory offerings to the tank divinity.

One of the chief drawbacks to enjoyment at Minneri and also at Polonaruwa is the plague of ticks, which, in the dry weather in the middle of the year, are a serious nuisance, but are not very plentiful from the middle of January to the middle of March—the best time for making the expedition. Strong carbolic soap is the best preventive. Returning to the road to Polonaruwa, the traveller will have four miles to go before arriving at the picturesque village and tank of Giritalé (Giritaláwa) where there is a small unfurnished bungalow ; and nine miles more will bring him to Topávewa (Polonaruwa) where he will find a similar bungalow (unfurnished). Permission to use these bungalows must be obtained from the Government Agent, Anuradhapura. The topography of the place is not difficulty, as nearly all the ruins lie in a straight line due north of the tank ; one or two, however, are not so easy to find ; and a guide had better be procured from the village, who will be well paid with 50 cents (8 annas) for the day.

It should be premised here that the following remarks upon the ruins are purely tentative. They are the result

of a sojourn of a few weeks made by the author several
years ago, when Archælogical discovery was in its infancy
in Ceylon.   The place is about to be " taken up " scienti-
fically by the Archæological Commissioner, and doubtless
the result of his investigations will throw a fuller light
on the problems and nomenclature of the ruins, and neces-
sitate the re-writing of this chapter.

Leaving the Gansabawa bungalow, the road passes
on the right a collection of stunted pillars which mark the
site of the great Durbar-hall, standing on a slight eminence.
The pillars are all ornamented, and many of them bear
traces of an inscription.   From this spot was taken the
beautifully-carved stone lion which is now in the Colombo
Museum.   Between these pillars and the Gansabawa is
a shapeless mass of brick-work with a small "pokuna"
below it, which still awaits identification and explanation.

The next point to be visited is the "kotuwa," or fort ;
a grim, roofless pile of brick-work, with walls about 25 ft.
high by 3 ft. thick, overgrown with enormous fig trees.
Below it is a much smaller building of a similar shape.
The identification of this structure and its appendages is
by no means clear.   It is also called, by local tradition,
" the king's prison" ; and all that can be said is, that it is
about as like a prison as a fort.   Due east of this lies the
" pattirippuwa," or pavilion, an oblong building measuring 75 ft. by 36 ft.   The wall which surrounds the platform, about 9 ft. high, is formed of large granite slabs, and
divided into terraces : each slab being decorated with bold
carvings of elephants, lions and gods.   The stones which
form the footway of each terrace are ornamented with a
delicate flower-border, and the pillars which stand on the
platform itself bear the flower-vase and the lotus pattern,

The stairways to the north and south are similar to those at Anuradhapura; only the griffins and lions assume larger proportions. About 100 yards to the east is a similar but smaller building, possibly the royal bathing pavilion; the base is ornamented with a fine façade of lions over ogee moulding. Close to it is the "kumára pokuna," or king's bathing-pond; a square paved tank with two entrances. On the western side are two stone spouts carved into crocodiles' heads; and in the centre of the tank lies the round stone on which the King sat while his attendants performed the necessary offices of ablution. Near it are three upright lions, which perhaps supported it, and various other broken carvings.

Proceeding northwards, and passing by a " sannas," or inscribed stone, on the left, a quarter-of-a-mile's walk will bring the visitor to the "Daladá Máligáwa"—the gem of Polonaruwa. This temple, as its name implies, was built to receive the sacred Tooth of Buddha when it was brought from Anuradhapura, by King Kirti Nissanga, about A D. 1198. It is still in wonderful preservation : the clear-cut figures and mouldings on the granite have suffered little from time; and though most of the roof has fallen in, the walls have been very little displaced. The building, which is Hindu in design, consists of an outer quadrangle, and an inner and innermost shrine. The inner shrine still retains its flat roof; and near the left wall is a curious square stone with a round hole pierced in it, probably a "Yóni stone". The innermost shrine, in which the Tooth was probably kept, bears traces of having had a conical or octagonal roof; and near the right wall may be seen the small stone drain which carried off the water after the washing of the sacred relic. In the outer quadrangle there is an inscribed stone near the north wall, the inscription running round all four sides, leaving a blank square in the centre ; and near it is an oblong stone pierced with 14 diamond-shaped holes. There are also the remains of two grotesque supporters, and several other carvings ; and near the eastern entrance various broken stone figures have been collected, which were found in the jungle close to the temple. The pillars round the outside of the inner shrines are quite unique, with their spreading capitals, and square bases finished off with cobra heads. Notice also the small external shrines on the south and west side ; and on the north, the spout and square receptacle which carried off the ablution water from the Holy of Holies.

North of the Daladá lies the Thupáráma, a large oblong brick building with an outer quadrangle and an inner vaulted chamber, over which is a low square tower. A bold frieze of lions runs round the base of the building. The principal entrance is to the east, and there is a smaller one to the north, and several narrow windows bisected by round stone pillars. Through these the thickness of the walls, which exceeds five feet, can be seen. The lofty entrance into the inner chamber is a remarkable specimen of a false arch, the horizontal layers of brick gradually approaching one another to form it. In a recess on the south side of this arch are the remains of a stairway, up which it is possible to scramble to the top of the building and the base of the tower.*

* Sir E. Tennent's account of this part of Polonaruwa is very puzzling. The picture he gives (vol. ii., p. 587, ed. 4) exactly corresponds to tho Thupáráma, while the letter-press describes it as the King's Palace, with which it in no way agrees ; and speaks of "several chambers" in it, no trace of which is now left.

Nearly opposite is the Wata Dágé ("round relic house"), a curious circular edifice standing on a raised mound, with four highly-carved staircases and a low stone terrace with an ornamental wall surrounding a tall circular wall of brick. The main entrance was apparently to the south; and near it are some pillars which mark the site of the "Mura-gé," or guard-house. The flower pattern in high relief which is carved on each of the huge slabs that form the outer wall of the terraces is quite unique; and this pattern is repeated in open work on a smaller slab at the top of the eastern stairway. There is a good moonstone to the south of building; and a very well-preserved series of lions and grotesque men running round the base; and a long inscription near the eastern entrance. Inside there is very little to be seen except the ruins of a dágoba, a broken sedent statue of Buddha, and an oblong stone vith diamond-shaped holes in it The Mahawanso mentions that Kitsen Kisdás, who reigned A.D. 1187, erected a temple of a circular form for the sacred Tooth, which perhaps may be the "Wata Dágé."

Close to the "Wata Dágé," and to the north of it, is the "Ata Dágé," or house of eight relics; which, though now greatly dilapidated, bears signs of having been most profusely ornamented. It was apparently an oblong building, with two chambers and an outer enclosure; on the south wall there is an elaborate plaster frieze of dancers and tom-tom beaters; and on the east side there is a window bisected by a round pillar and decorated with the goose emblem. Near the outer wall of this building, on the eastern side, lies a huge monolith known as the "galpota" or stone book, as it resembles a volume of olas, or palmyra leaves. It measures 28 ft. long, 5 ft. broad, and 2 ft. 5 inches thick, and bears a long inscription,

which records the virtues and great deeds of King
Nissaṇga, who reigned A.D. 1192-1201. It tells how,
when the King traversed a dry desert, and wished for
water, an unexpected cloud instantly poured down an
abundant shower—how that the State elephant no sooner
saw the king, than he raised a shout of triumph and took
him on his back—how his Majesty wearing his crown
and being decorated with the royal ornaments, caused
himself, as well as the chief queens and his son and
daughter, to be weighed in a balance every year; and by
bestowing five times their weight of goods on priests,
Brahmins and the poor, made them happy and caused a
constant supply of rain.   Finally, it states that this stone
is the one which the chief minister caused the strong men
of King Nissaṇga to bring from the mountain of Mihintalé
at Anuradhapura.   It is not clear why it was thought
worth while to carry this enormous slab a distance of
more than eighty miles.   The inscription is surrounded
by a moulding of geese ; and a design formed of elephants,
geese, and the sitting Buddha is to be found at either end
of the stone.

The " Sat-mahal-prasáda," or palace of seven stories,
rises up close to it, The object of this building is not
very clear ; but it is in excellent preservation ; several of
the statues that ornamented each story are still visible ;
and by creeping into the east entrance, the remains of a
staircase, which probably led to the summit, can be seen.
The base of the building is 28 ft. 6 in. square.

There is a very curious collection of low pillars to
the west, known as the "Bana Sáláwa," or preaching hall.
The area it covers, measuring 32 ft. by 27 ft., is surrounded
by pillars with conical capitals, each pierced to receive

three stone bars, which, in one instance, remain perfect
The resemblance to the post and rail ornaments of the
" Sanchi Tope" in India, the oldest Buddhist monument
extant, is remarkable. The remains of a beautifully ornamented inscription and of several inscribed pillars of a
unique shape, have been found in the centre of the
enclosure.

Due east of this group of ruins lies a solitary building
known as the " Vishnu Dewále," approached by a narrow
jungle path about quarter-of-a-mile in length. This temple
closely resembles the · " Daladá Máligáwa" in conception
and ornamentation, though it is not nearly so elaborate·
The small outer chamber or porch is very much broken,
and access to the inner shrine is prevented by the intoler-
able stench of the bats. This shrine is surmounted by an
octagonal roof in good preservation; and a long Tamil
inscription runs along the outside of the southern wall.

Returning to the Sat-mahal-prasáda and first group
of ruins, the path runs northward through jungle for
about half-a-mile, and then emerges on the Rankot (golden
spire) dágoba, which appears to have been built by the
second Queen of Rája Párákrama Báhu, between A D. 1154
and 1186, and to have been added to, and supplied with
basement chapels by, King Kirti Nissanga ten years later.
It is nearly 200 ft. in height, with a diameter of about
180 ft. Eight small shrines surround the base, with
conical roofs, and a plain interior; and between each
pair is a larger structure which perhaps supported an
image or relic. The spire of the dágoba is very perfect;
and the statues which ·surround the drum are plainly
visible with field glasses. On the south-east side there
are the remains of a brick figure of Buddha, about 8 ft.

6 in. high and of the arched roof under which it stood ;
and to the north there is an old well. About 300 yards to
the east there is a moulded and inscribed monolith, 3 ft.
4 in. square by 2 ft. 9 in. high.

Still proceeding northwards, the path leads to the
Jétawanáráma, the most imposing of the Polonaruwan
structures. It is oblong in shape and about 150 ft. in
length ; and is divided into two large chambers, the inner
one being broader than the outer, The decoration of the
exterior of the side walls, which are nearly 80 ft. high,
is very elaborate and strictly Hindu in its character.
The main entrance is to the east : opposite to it are some
decorated pillars which are locally said to mark the site
of the Gansabawa or tribunal where minor offences were
tried ; but this is improbable. The entrance to the shrine
is flanked by two polygonal turrets, and was orginally
guarded by two grotesque figures in high relief. The
flight of stone steps (each 20 ft. long) is elaborately carved,
and there is an inscription on the near side of one of the
janitors. There was evidently a gateway between the
outer and inner shrines ; and at the western end of the
latter stands a gigantic brick-work figure of Buddha, nearly
60 ft. high, which was originally coated with chunam. A
small row of windows low down in the wall appears to
have been the only means of admitting light into this
shrine ; and Tennent* conjectures with some probability
that by means of a window situated above the entrance
to the inner shrine, and invisible from below, a ray of
light was thrown full upon the face of the statue, giving
it a mysterious halo amid the surrounding gloom. There

* Vol. II., Pt. x , ch. 1., p. 593.

is a similar "trick of light" in the pagoda known as the
cave of Ananda at Paganmyo on the Irawaddy.

Close to the Jétawanáráma stands a small dágoba
known as the Kiri (milk) Vihára, so-called from the white
chunam with which it was originally covered. It is about
100 ft. in height, with a diameter of about 70 ft. ; but it
does not compare favourably with the proportions of the
Rankot dágoba.

Another stretch of jungle intervenes between this
dágoba and the "Gal Vihára," which lies to the north.
Just before reaching this latter, notice a curious stone on
the right, close to the path, which is said to have been
used by the painters to grind their colours in. The "Gal
Vihára" (rock temple) consists of three figures of heroic
size, and a shrine containing a smaller figure ; they are
all carved out of the same abrupt boulder of dark granite.
The southernmost figure represents the sedent Buddha
in the conventional attitude, and is 15 ft. high above the
pedestal. The background of the figure is elaborately
carved : from the squares of the pilasters, dragons' heads
project ; and from the mouth of each issues a small lion.
Higher up are representations of Hindu pagodas. The
pedestal on which the figure sits has a bold frieze of lions
alternating with a curious emblem which may be a pair of
dragons' heads reversed. Next to this figure comes the
shrine, which is cut out of the solid rock, and contains a
rock-cut sedent figure of Buddha 4 ft. 7 in. high, seated
on a pedestal 3 ft. high. The background of the figure is
profusely decorated with "deviyòs" (minor divinities)
bearing torches, grotesque lions, lotuses, etc., and the
pedestal of the statue has a frieze of alternate lions and
dragons' heads. The whole has unfortunately been much

disfigured by modern attempts to paint it on the part of a priest whose enterprize was in advance of his taste.

Between the shrine and the upright figure, the face of the rock has been smoothed to receive a long inscription of no particular interest. It consists of 51 lines of writing, and measures 13 ft. 9 in. The erect figure, which is 23 ft. high, and stands on a circular pedestal ornamented with lotus leaves, represents "Ananda," the favourite disciple of Buddha, grieving for the loss, or rather the translation, of his master. The figure has generally been taken for a Buddha, but erroneously, as it is obviously not in the conventional attitude of the standing Buddha; and further, the Mahawaṇso distinctly states that King Parákrama Báhu "caused statues of Buddha in a sitting and a lying posture to be carved out of the same rock," making no mention of an upright statue of Buddha.

The reclining figure of Buddha is by far the finest of the three. It measures 46 ft. in length, and has suffered little from the ravages of time. The expression of complete repose upon the face, the listless attitude of the arm and hand, the carefully arranged folds of the robe, together with the extreme stillness of the surrounding jungle, combine to form a wonderful realization of the ideal Nirvána.

One more ruin remains to be visited. It is known as the "Demala Mahá Séya," and lies nearly half-a-mile to the north of the "Gal Vihára." It is a large oblong building, very much in the style of the Jétawanáráma; its walls being covered with grotesque Hindu emblems and figures. Notice particularly on the south wall the frieze of uneasy human figures which appear to be supporting the building; and on the north wall the distorted, haggard figures of

the fakirs.   The entrance appears to have been to the
east ; but the whole front has fallen in, and not an aperture
is left whereby any idea can be formed of the interior of
the shrine.   From the summit, a fine view can be obtained
of the surrounding country ; the mountain known as
Gunner's Quoin forming a conspicuous object to the
south-east.

A walk of about a mile-and-a-quarter from the Gansabawa bungalow to the south-east, partly along the margin
of the lake, leads to a very interesting statue of King
Parákrama Báhu, the one great monarch of the Polonaruwan epoch, and the constructor of nearly all its great
temples and monuments.   It is 11 ft. 6 in. high, and is
cut out of the solid rock.   The King is turning his back
to his capital, and holds in his hands the open book of
the law ; and the position and attitude may possibly be
meant to express the idea that there is more consolation
in religious meditation than in the erection of many
dágobas and palaces.   The expression of pride and dis-
content upon the face is so real and distinctive, that one
is tempted to think it was a study from the life.

PART III.
MISCELLANEOUS.

MISCELLANEOUS.

ARRIVAL OF MAILS AT ANURADHAPURA.

Mails from Matale, Kandy, Colombo and
    stations on that line arrive at   -   8   P.M.
Northern line mails (Jaffna, etc.) arrive at -   5   A.M.
Mails from Mihintale -   - do -   4   P.M.

DESPATCH OF MAILS FROM ANURADHAPURA

Mails for Colombo, Matale, &c. close 5 A.M. & despt. 6 A.M.
    Do Mihintale -   do 6 A.M.   do 6 A.M.
    Do Jaffna line -   do 8 P.M.   do 9 P.M.

TELEGRAMS

Ordinary Telegrams are accepted between 7 A.M. and 8
P.M. except on Sundays, Christmas day, New Year's
day, Good Friday and Queen's Birthday, when they
are accepted between 7 A.M. and 9 A.M. and from 4
P.M. to 6 P.M.

Urgent Telegrams are accepted at all hours for offices that
are open at the time such telegrams are tendered for
transmission.

MONEY ORDERS.

are accepted between 10 A.M. and 3 P.M. except on Saturdays and Government holidays, when the hours of business are from 10 A.M. to 1 P.M.

Above rule applies to Savings Bank as well.

ANURADHAPURA RESTHOUSE.

The undermentioned established charges have been approved by His Excellency the Governor, under Clause No. 19 of Ordinance No. 10 of 1861, (see Colonial Secretary's letter No. 20 of 6th October 1893) :—

	R.	c.
For occupation for 24 hours or under, each person	1	00
For a bed in addition to charge for occupation of Resthouse, each night	0	75
For a couch do do do	0	50
For stable for 24 hours or under, each horse	0	25
For coach house for 24 hours or under, each conveyance	0	25
For each bullock stabled for 24 hours or less	0	25
Each carriage or cart inside the compound for 24 hours or less	0	25
For each bullock inside the Compound for 24 hours or less	0	$12\frac{1}{2}$

The Resthouse-keeper will supply bed and table linen, if required, for which he is entitled to charge :—

	R.	c.
For sheets and pillow cases, each night -	0	50
For table linen, each day - -	0	25

It is left to the liberality of travellers to remunerate the Resthouse-keeper for any services he may be called upon to render in the way of cooking, procuring supplies, water, &c.

OTHER RESTHOUSES.

The undermentioned established charges have been approved by His Excellency the Governor, under Clause No. 19 of Ordinance No. 10 of 1861 (see Colonial Secretary's letter No. 20 of 6th October 1893):—

	R.	c.
For occupation for a night, or day and night, each person	0	50
For occupation for a day only for any time, each person	0	25
For a bed in addition to charge for occupation of Resthouse, each night	0	75
For a couch do do do	0	50
For a horse for 24 hours or under	0	25
For a coach house for 24 hours or under, each conveyance	0	25
For each carriage or cart halted inside the compound for 24 hours or less	0	25
For each bullock inside the compound for 24 hours or less	0	$12\frac{1}{2}$
For each bullock stabled for 24 hours or less	0	25

The Resthouse-keeper will supply Bed and Table linen for which he is entitled to charge :—

	R.	c.
For sheets and pillow case, each night	0	50
For table linen each day	0	25

It is left to the liberality of travellers to remunerate the Resthouse-keeper for any services he may be called upon to render in the way of cooking, procuring supplies, water, &c.

CENTRAL ROAD MAIL COACH TIME AND FARE TABLE.

STATIONS.	Europeans.		Burghers, Native Lawyers & Officers.		Natives.		APPROXIMATE	
							Time of Arrival.	Time of Departure.
	R.	c.	R.	c.	R.	c.		
Jaffna ..								2-30 P.M.
Chavakachcheri	1	50	1	00	0	75	4-40 P.M.	4-45 P.M.
Pallai	3	00	2	25	1	50	7 P.M.	7-30 P.M.
Elephant Pass	4	00	3	00	2	00	9-15 P.M.	9-30 P.M.
Eranamadu	5	75	4	25	2	75	1-30 A.M.	1-35 A.M.
Panikankulam	7	50	5	25	3	62	4-55 A.M.	5 A.M.
Mankulam	8	50	6	00	4	00	—	—
Kanagarayankulam	10	00	7	00	4	50	8-20 A.M.	8-30 A.M.
Rambaikulam	11	25	8	50	5	25	12-50 A.M.	1-20 P.M.
Vanniya	14	00	10	00	6	00	4-35 P.M.	5 P.M.
Madawachchi	17	00	12	00	7	50	10-40 P.M.	10 45 P.M.
Anuradhapura	20	00	14	00	9	00	5 A.M.	6 A.M.
Matale	30	00	17	50	10	00	8 P.M.	—
Every additional mile	00	25	00	18	00	10	—	—

From Anuradhapura to

STATIONS.	Europeans.		Burghers, Native Lawyers & Officers.		Natives.		Time of Arrival.	Time of Departure.
Tirappanai	3	00	2	00	1	50	8-30 A.M.	8-35 A.M.
Maradankadawela	5	00	3	00	2	00	—	—
Kekkaravai	6	00	4	00	2	50	10-30 A.M.	10-35 A.M.
Dambulla	9	00	6	00	4	00	1 P.M.	1-30 P.M.
Nalanda	12	00	8	00	5	50	4-30 P.M.	4-35 P.M.
Matale	15	00	10	00	7	00	8 P.M.	—

CENTRAL ROAD MAIL COACH TIME AND FARE TABLE,—(*Continued.*)

STATIONS.	Europeans.		Burghers, Native Lawyers and officers.		Natives.		APPROXIMATE	
							Time of Arrival.	Time of Departure.
	R.	c.	R.	c.	R.	c.		
Matale								8 A.M.
Nalanthai	3	00	2	00	1	50	10-25 A.M.	10-30 A.M.
Dambulla	6	00	4	00	3	00	12-30 A.M.	1 P.M.
Kekkaravai	9	00	6	00	4	50	2-15 P.M.	2-20 P.M.
Maradankadawela	10	00	7	00	5	00	4 P.M.	4-5 P.M.
Tirappanai	12	00	8	00	6	00	5 P.M.	5-5 P.M.
Anuradhapura	15	00	10	00	7	00	8 P.M.	9 P.M.
Jaffna	30	00	17	50	10	00	8 P.M.	—
Every additional mile	00	25	00	18	00	10	—	—

From Anuradhapura to

STATIONS.	Europeans.		Burghers, Native Lawyers and officers.		Natives.		Time of Arrival.	Time of Departure.
Madawachchi	3	00	2	00	1	50	2-45 A.M.	3 A.M.
Vavuniya	6	00	4	00	3	00	8 A.M.	8-30 A.M.
Rambaikulam	8	75	5	50	3	75	11-45 A.M.	12-15 A.M.
Kanagarayankulam	10	00	7	00	4	50	4-15 P.M.	4-30 P.M.
Mankulam	11	50	8	00	5	00	—	—
Panikankulam	12	00	8	75	5	37	7-50 P.M.	8-30 P.M.
Eranamadu	14	25	9	75	6	25	11-50 P.M.	11-55 P.M.
Elephant Pass	16	00	11	00	7	00	4 A.M.	4-15 A.M.
Pallai	17	00	11	75	7	50	6 A.M.	6-30 A.M.
Chavakachcheri	18	50	13	00	8	25	8-45 A.M.	8-50 A.M.
Jaffna	20	00	14	00	9	00	11 A.M	—

MAIL COACH RULES.

THE MATALE-JAFFNA MAIL COACH Proprietors in thanking the public for the patronage they have received, beg to give notice that they have made every arrangement to suit the travelling Public, and the following is published for general information.

SEATS should be booked upon twenty-four hours' previous notice and whole Coach three days at least.

WHOLE COACH to consist of three passengers, and luggage not to exceed one hundredweight (1 cwt.) and can be engaged only between the following stations, viz., Matale-Dambulla, Matale-Anuradhapura, Anuradhapura-Jaffna, Matale-Jaffna, Jaffna-Elephant Pass, Jaffna-Kanagarayankulam, Jaffna-Vavuniya, Jaffna-Anuradhapura, Anuradhapura-Matale, and Jaffna-Matale.

CHALLENGE OF SEATS can be made only at Matale, Dambulla, Anuradhapura, Vavuniya and Jaffna. Any ordinary seat can be challenged from the last No. upwards according to the order tickets are issued, by any individual who is willing to tender the amount of EUROPEAN FARE for the same. Challenge can be made for the whole Coach if there are under five passengers travelling through. Persons desirous to engage the whole Coach from any intermediate station must pay for the whole Coach from such intermediate station to the end of the Journey, if on the day in question there are any passengers in the Coach who have booked their journey right through.

In the event of the Coach being engaged; no challenge will be accepted.

LUGGAGE.—Europeans allowed 30 lbs. free of charge, Burghers, Native Lawyers and Officers 20 lbs. and others 15 lbs. each.

INTERMEDIATE STATIONS.—The following are the charges, viz., Europeans 25 cts., Burghers, Native Lawyers and Officers 18 cts., and Natives 10 cts. per mile.

PARCELS RATES.—Five cents per lb. all along the line.

PACKAGES.—None other than those which could, with convenience, be packed in the Coach, will be accepted. This refers to size and weight.

SPECIAL RESERVATION.—The proprietors reserve a seat for the establishment and the Postal Department all along the line and at all times.

THE JAFFNA COACHING COY.

Proprietors.

THE RAILWAY TIME TABLE BETWEEN COLOMBO, KANDY AND MATALE.

UP.

STATIONS.		WEEK DAYS.							SUNDAYS.	
		A.M.	A.M.	A.M.	A.M.	P.M.	P.M.	P.M.	A.M.	P.M.
Colombo Terminus	Dep.	6·0	7·30	7·40	..	1·50	6·0	Mail*	7·0	3·0
Maradana Junction	..	6·6	7·34	7·45	9·0	1·55	6·5	9·40	7·5	8·5
Kelaniya	..	6·16	..	7·54	9·8	2·4	6·15	...	7·15	8·15
Hunupitiya	..	6·24	...	8·2	—	2·11	6·22	...	7·22	3·22
Ragama	..	6·37	..	8·15	..	2·24	6·33	..	7·33	3·33
Heneratgoda	..	7·5	...	8·48	...	2·45	6·53	...	7·55	3·55
Veyangoda	.	7·28	8·25	9·8	...	3·5	7·13	10·33	8·14	4·16
Mirigama	..	8·0	...	9·30	..	3·26	7·36	...	8·38	4·39
Ambepussa	..	8·13	...	9·50	...	3·38	7·49	...	8·51	4·52
Alawwa	.	8·29	..	10·6	...	3·53	8·5	..	9·7	5·8
Polgahawela	Arr	8·42	9·12	10·19	...	4·5	8·17	11·35	9·19	5·20
Do	Dep	9·16	...	...	...	4·11	8·19	11·40	9·23	5·23
Rambukkana	..	9·38	..	..	..	4·38	8·45	12·5	9·45	5·46
Kadugannawa	..	10·35	...			5·35	9·52	1·10	10·43	6·46
Peradeniy Junctiona	Arr.	10·55	..		P.M.	5·56	10·9	1·28	11·0	7·3
Do do	Dep.	11·3	...		1·35	...	...	1·15	11·9	7·11
Kandy	Arr.	11.15	..		..	6·15	10·25	1·45	11·20	7.25

Between Kandy and Matale.

		A.M.	A.M.	P.M.	P.M.	A.M.	A.M.	P.M.	P.M.
						SUNDAYS.			
Kandy	Dep.	5·55	11·25	3·0	6·25	5·55	11·30	2·45	7·35
Mahaiyawa	..	6·0	11·30	2·5	6·30	6·0	11·36	2·51	7·41
Katugastota	...	6·12	11·42	3·15	6·40	6·12	11·49	3·4	7·54
Wattegama	...	6·28	11·56	3·30	6·55	6·28	12·4	3·19	8·9
Ukuwela	..	6·49	12·18	3·50	7·15	6·49	12·24	3·39	8·29
Matale	Arr.	7·0	12·30	4·0	7·25	7·0	12·35	3·50	8·40

DOWN.

STATIONS.		WEEK DAYS.				SUNDAYS.			
		A.M.	A.M.	P.M.	P.M.	A.M.	A.M.	P.M.	P.M.
Matale	Dep.	5·55	9·20	12·50	4·25	5·55	9·30	12·55	4·15
Ukuwela	...	6·6	9·31	1·1	4·35	6·7	9·42	1·7	4·27
Wattegama	..	6·27	9·53	1·23	4·57	6·29	10·4	1·29	4·49
Katugastota	...	6·40	10·8	1·38	5·15	6·43	10·18	1·43	5·3
Mahaiyawa	...	6·53	10·22	1·52	5·25	6·55	10·30	1·55	5·15
Kandy	Arr.	7·00	10·30	2·0	5·30	7·0	10·35	2·0	5·20

Between Kandy and Colombo.

		A.M.	A.M.	A.M.	A.M.	P.M.	P.M.	A.M.	P.M.	P.M.
								SUNDAYS.		
Kandy	Dep.	5·0	7·10	10·35		2·5	...	7·10	1·5	..
Peradeniya Junction	..	5·17	7·28	11·9		2·17	...	7·28	1·26	..
Kadugannawa	..	5·40	7·49	11·31		2·47	2·35	7·49	1·48	2·35
Rambukkana	..	6·49	8·56	12·35†		3·50	3·35	8·56	2·52	3·35
Polgahawela	Arr.	7·6	9·13	12·52		4·6	3·55	9·14	3·8	3·55
Do	Dep.	7·10	9·15	12.54	1·10	4·10	3·55	9·20	3·13	3·52
Alawwa	...	7·25	9·28	..	1·23	...	...	9·32	3·26	..
Ambepussa	..	7·43	9·45	..	1·44	...	..	9·47	3·42	..
Mirigama	...	7·55	9·59	...	1·56	..	...	10·0	3·56	...
Veyangoda	..	8·17	10·22	1·50	2·20	5·0	4·55	10·22	4·20	4·55
Henaratgoda	..	8·42	10·39	...	2·39	...		10·39	4·38	..
Ragama	..	9·5	11·0	2·30	3·13	...	...	11·0	5·0	...
Hunupitiya	..	9·16	11·11	..	3·25	...	...	11·13	5·12	...
Kelaniya	..	9·25	11·18		3·34	..	...	11·22	5·21	..
Maradana Junction	Arr.	9·33	11·26	2·52	3·43	5·50	5·55	11·31	5·30	5·50
Colombo	Arr.	9·45	11·38	3·0	3·50	6·0	6·5	11·40	5·40	6·0

* Passengers change Trains.   † p.m.